Love Your Life

Dad's Secrets to a Happy and Well Balanced Life

David Shuley

ISBN: 9798634327990

For Ethan, Blake, Brooke, and Grace

Contents

Forward

Ethan Shuley (Oldest Son)

Some of the fondest memories I had with my dad were often traveling to my cross country and track races. It was one of the few times where we could spend time together just one on one. I remember during my junior track season, I scheduled a particular race down in Richmond, Virginia. My dad never questioned my desire to find a fast race to qualify for the national championships. He was willing to take off work and drive me down 7 and a half hours both ways to run for a mere 9 minutes and 11 seconds. I not only enjoyed those years because of the quality time I got to spend with my dad, but also because he always took the opportunity to support me and my other siblings in all of our ambitions wholeheartedly with his time.

My Dad loves his life and his family. I cannot express into words how much he has sacrificed for me and my other siblings to become the people we are today. When I look back at my childhood and teenage years, what I have come to appreciate is how much time my dad would spend time with us. I attribute my strong relationship with my dad now to all the small moments I had with him growing up such as sitting around the table as a family for dinner or playing soccer in the basement. His commitment to spending time with his family was 100 times more evident of his love and care for me and my siblings than any compliment or phrase words could ever express. While to some people spending this much time might be viewed as a sacrifice at the expense of success in a career or other accomplishment, I never felt this was the case with my dad. I always saw joy in him when he was able to spend time with me.

Blake Shuley (son)

My dad has always been one to achieve the success he desires because of the personal discipline in his life. What I have seen is he personally enjoys the challenges that come his way.

Ever since my dad was young, one of his biggest passions was running. His high school running career showed promise, but various injuries limited his success. These running injuries continued to plague him as an adult, limiting his ability to train and keeping him out of several races that he had set his sights on. He even adopted cycling and raced for 10 years in an effort to stay active and in shape. But his passion for running never left him.

Finally, many years later, we watched my dad attempt another return to running. This attempt was fraught with challenges as the prior injuries continued to haunt him. Yet he persevered, and even hired a personal trainer in an effort to keep his body injury-free. He trained with ups and downs until finally his personal discipline paid off. His goal of running another marathon (the 2nd of his life) became reality when he completed the St. George Marathon. Since then he has completed a 3rd marathon and qualified to run in the Boston Marathon.

Looking back on these years of struggle, I think there are many times when my dad could have lost hope. But his personal discipline—that quality I've come to admire so much in my dad—brought him the success he was seeking.

Brooke Shuley (daughter)

"It's nice to be nice." This is something my dad has always said to me growing up. I think that one of the reasons my dad loves life so much is because he is so charitable to those around him.

One year, a couple of weeks before Christmas, my dad asked my siblings and me if we'd like to donate one of our Christmas gifts to a charity or organization of our choice. We had always received three gifts in the past, but he wanted us to have the choice to be nice during the Christmas season and give one of them away. I had always been very thankful and sometimes felt guilty for the great gifts we were given, so when hearing this idea, my siblings and I all decided to do it.

My dad has always been the best example of kindness and charity, and not just during the Christmas season. I have always seen the way he strives to be the "friendliest person in the room" or in any situation, and I know that this is how he loves his life. When you serve others and are nice to them, it leaves you with great happiness. That is definitely one thing I have learned from my dad.

Grace Shuley (daughter)

My dad is the master of the sugar coat. He's made many plans happen with this trick of his. "Want to go to your friend's house? Oh sure, I just have one tiny stop." Which then leads to visiting someone from our church to share the gospel. Or when he asks for a "little bite" and then takes a massive chomp out of my sandwich. Don't get me wrong; he's a great man. He just likes to make things sound better or less awful than they really are. I never saw this as a big issue, just something to keep in mind in case he wanted me to do something outside my comfort zone.

Three years ago, our family took a trip to Iceland. After about a week of being there, my dad mentioned a hike right next to our little hotel. He sugarcoated the description by saying that there were 21 waterfalls over the course of 8 miles. Based on previous experience with my dad's explanation of things, I wasn't totally on board. He downplayed the fact that in order to get to the trailhead, we had to climb "the Stairmaster." It was about 15 switchback staircases up the face of a cliff. Anyway, the hike was off to a tiresome start, but I was already counting the waterfalls. My uncle Chris and aunt Rena had joined us a few days prior and were trudging along with us through the hike. After successfully counting all twenty-one waterfalls, my dad informed the group that we had to speed up if we were going to catch the bus that would take us home.

At that point, I grew skeptical of how long this hike really was. We came across a board with a map on it. A large 29-km was stretched along the bottom of the map and a star at 13 km (8 mi.). Our eyes widened as we soon realized that to reach the bus, we had to cross another 16 km over the top of the mountain Eyjafjallajokull and back down the other side. This was an 18-mile hike over a mountain that had erupted 7 years prior to our hike. That was more than my dad's original explanation.

Kelby Losack once said "Creativity's too big a pill; the truth's too hard to swallow. Sprinkle sugar in a straight line and we'll all inhale and follow." That was the painful truth in our situation. We all tightened our shoelaces, strapped our backpacks tighter, and kept on moving. We eventually reached the wilderness bus station after hiking through a vast Martian land, cat backs, a foggy mountain pass, snowfields, and cliff-ridden chained mountain peaks. The whole adventure had taken us 8 hours. We made the bus with 30 minutes to spare. My dad sugarcoated the heck out of this day, yet this hike is now my all-time favorite. Sometimes we have to appreciate the sugarcoat because it gets us to do the things that we don't want to do but should do.

I'll be straightforward with you, no sugarcoat, this is a book you're going to want to read.

Introduction

When I was in college, I came home each summer to work and save money. My highest paying summer job was working as a busboy at the Steamboat Steakhouse. This restaurant was part of a permanent barge sitting on the shore of the Ohio River, which had a spectacular view of the Cincinnati skyline. It was an above average American restaurant with an above average price.

When I applied for the job I had no experience in restaurants. The only food establishment I had worked at was McDonalds. I didn't drink so I had little knowledge about alcohol. Heck, I wasn't even a coffee drinker, so I was useless helping patrons with beverage choices. With my limited experience, I could not be a waiter, but I supported them as a busboy. My job was to come up to the tables toward the end of the meal and clear the patron's plates and ask them if they would like a cup of coffee. Then when everyone had left I got the table ready for the next customer.

One day I had a gentleman who I had just cleared his plate motion for me to come back over to him. When I got there, he asked me if I had any mayonnaise for his coffee? I said, "Sure I will get you some." As I walked away, I pictured mayonnaise floating in his coffee. It sounded disgusting. I am not a coffee drinker, but I would have never thought those two things mixed. I guess I lived in Kentucky, which was my excuse.

I went back to the kitchen to ask for a side of mayonnaise and brought it out to him. When I placed it on the table he smiled at me, chuckled and said, "What is this? No, you didn't hear me right, I need some bay leaves." I was embarrassed, and quickly said with a laugh, "So sorry, I was wondering why you would put mayonnaise in your coffee."

I then went back to the kitchen to get a side of bay leaves. Again, not being a coffee drinker I tried to imagine putting bay leaves in coffee. I knew my mother used it for her spaghetti sauce, so I imagined it must add some sort of flavor. But I still felt that sounded weird.

I got my side of bay leaves and walked out to the man. As I placed the bay leaves in front of him he just sat in disbelief and shook his head. He asked me, "You don't have a clue what Bailey's cream is, do you?" I looked at him like a naive child and said, "No, I have never heard of it." He said, "It is a liqueur for your coffee. Go talk to someone at the bar."

I walked over to the bar with my tail between my legs and asked for some Baileys. They gave it to me and I took it over to him. He smiled at me like a proud papa who just witnessed his son walk for the first time. He then said, "Thank you" and resumed talking to his family. I darted away and said to myself, "I am such an idiot."

That was probably not the only person that I have encountered in my life who has thought of me as an idiot. I am sure there are many. Like all of us, I had a lot to learn then and I am still learning, but at this point there are so many experiences that I can just laugh about. I have learned much through what life has thrown at me. So what I can say after 51 years on this earth is: this idiot feels happy. I love my life. I feel fortunate to be able to live the life that I live and to have the people I have around me. In fact, I have been blessed with most of what this world has to offer. I have built a successful, nationally-recognized financial planning firm. I have traveled the world from Bora Bora to Norway, from Japan to Russia. I have raced in marathons and extreme bike races; I have led congregations and humbly served in adventurous Christian mission trips. I have been blessed with many good friends. Most importantly, I married an amazing woman and together we have raised four incredible children. I simply love life. I feel so fortunate.

Of course, my life hasn't been without difficulties and mistakes. I have had times of stress and problems. I have seen some truly difficult things. There are times that I feel my family is dysfunctional. I have had moments where I have said, "Why does this always happen to me?" Similarly, I believe there are times for each of us when it takes discipline to see the good that can come out of challenges. It takes discipline to be grateful. What I have learned through it all is everyone's life has meaning and purpose. We each have reason to be here. Personally, I have been blessed with wonderful people around me, and an abundance of fond moments that I can look back on with a smile. I wouldn't trade my life with anyone.

There are two reasons why I have decided to write this book. First, I want my kids to know what I feel are the most important secrets to living a meaningful and joyful life, the type of life that will direct them to happiness. I want them to love life and apply what I have learned so they can minimize the mistakes in their own lives.

Second, I want my children to know stories from my life that have helped teach me these principles. My hope is that the stories will illuminate the principles to help clearly convey their importance.

I have noticed that many different authors have written about what makes a successful life. I have learned a lot through the reading of these good books. But I feel that there are many things to be said that have not been widely published. There is a higher way of living. It isn't all unique and new concepts. Some are old concepts that seem to be lost in today's society. But these things have had a huge impact on my life. I am sure my way is not the only way. But my way has created a life I love.

After writing a few chapters of this book, I realized that this might be helpful for more than just my family. I believe these principles are of universal value and can be profitable to a wide and varied audience. So this book originally intended for my family, is also a book for the world. I hope all can glean from its ideas and have it impact their lives for good. I want everyone to love their lives to the fullest.

CHAPTER 1

Surround Yourself with Eagles

"Surround yourself with only people who are going to lift you higher." —Oprah Winfrey

Growing up in the Seattle area, I had a fascination with the tall, full evergreen trees that were scattered throughout my neighborhood. The most prominent trees are the Western Red Cedar. These trees are one of the most important resources to the area. They provide shelter, firewood, food, medicine, wildlife habitat, and so much more. They can grow up to 200 feet tall and be almost 19 feet in diameter. They have large, thick branches close to the base of the tree that show off their beauty with deep, dark, green needles. Rough to the touch, the needles are compressed and scaly. There is an intoxicating aroma around these trees, reminiscent of a fresh cut Christmas tree. When I think of the beauty of the Northwest, I think of these magnificent evergreens.

My friends and I often gathered around the base of certain old overgrown trees where the branches near the base hung all the way to the ground. Their shelter provided a private haven in my particular neighborhood. The trees concealed us from everyone else. It was more than a shelter, you could not hear or see from outside the large bushy base. We could do whatever we wanted and no one would know, especially our parents. The trees protected our secrets from the world.

One day while hanging out inside the tree, one of my friends pulled out a small, clear, sandwich bag containing marijuana. The older kids from the street shared a stash of drugs in a box that had been buried in a random neighbor's yard. My friend had taken it out for us to have a smoke. At this moment, I really didn't know what to do. Growing up, I lived in a religious home and had been taught correct principles. I was a happy and respectful child inside my home, but I tried to be as cool as I could be with my friends. As I looked down at the substance, my thoughts were somewhat conflicted. My friend pulled out a pipe and some of the marijuana from the sandwich bag and then turned to light it up. After he had a puff, he passed me the pipe so I could take my turn. As I held the pipe in my hand, I pushed out any hesitation in my mind. Acceptance was more important than doing what I knew to be right. I brought the pipe to my mouth and let in the smoke. Immediately, I began to choke, so I passed the pipe over. I didn't know that I was supposed to inhale as I smoked. Consequently, I felt nothing.

As I returned home, I devised a plan to get rid of the lingering cannabis smell. I piled the toothpaste onto my brush and cleaned my mouth. I couldn't afford to let my parents find out. I brushed and brushed, then rinsed and brushed some more. Afterwards, I changed my clothes to keep any suspicious scent off my body. I assumed that when my mother did the laundry she wouldn't notice the difference from the usual stink of a boy. My plan worked. She never asked a single question. I was still her innocent little third grader.

Our "fun" didn't end there. We started to learn the art of shoplifting. We often stole food, candy, and sometimes fishing supplies at the local Fischer Drug store. We became good at it. Our philosophy was; grab whatever we wanted to steal and walk out with it in plain sight. We hoped people would blatantly see whatever we stole in our hands and assume that we had already paid for it. We did not put anything into our pockets nor try to conceal it in any way. Each time, we calmly walked out of the store with the candy in our hands. We did this multiple times with great success.

After one successful theft, we hid behind a stinky outdoor garbage can while waiting on the others to exit the store. Gradually, everyone met back up except my older brother. We continued to wait, but he never came back out. We wondered what we should do next. Meanwhile, my brother was still in the store. He had gone back to the manager's office and had asked the store manager to open a glass case. Inside contained a large slingshot.

The manager then opened the case and gave the slingshot to my brother. It was a prized possession. He would have been the envy of the neighborhood. Now my brother had to develop a plan. To make his escape, he remained in the store looking at other merchandise while holding the slingshot. Then he began to walk out hoping no one would notice. The store manager knew full well my brother's intentions and prevented him from leaving. He took my brother back into his office and called the police.

At the time, we had no idea what was going on. As we sat behind the garbage can, we decided to go back to find out what happened to my brother, only to be greeted by the police. The manager had apparently told the police that my brother had friends that had also shoplifted and might be coming back into the store. They immediately took us to the manager's office to be disciplined. My hair stood up on the back of my neck as we walked toward the office. I was scared to the core. Thoughts went through my mind, "This is real trouble." "What will the police do?" "What will my parents do?" I would soon find out.

The police called our parents and told them to come to the store to have a talk. When my parents arrived, I saw the look on my mom's face. She was so disappointed. She had no idea I could ever do such a thing. I felt horrible. My vision began to blur as tears filled my eyes. The police interrupted our moment and warned if we continued to steal, our lives in the future would be spent in jail. I had visions of my future at that moment that disturbed me. The experience scared me so much that I never stole again.

By the time I was in 4th grade, I had viewed porn magazines, smoked cigarettes, experimented with drugs, shoplifted, and been sent twice to the principal's office for swearing. All this occurred while in my home I lived a seemingly happy, fun filled, loving, religious, life with my parents and siblings. Even though they didn't find out too many details till later, my mom always said that before the age of ten were my most rebellious years. The cause, in my view, is I did what my friends were doing. When I was outside my home I felt the need to be accepted. I wanted to do what they did. Consequently, I had become like them. If nothing had changed, my path would have led me to a bad place.

We always had fun with the neighborhood gang. I am pictured with my sister and brother on the front row.

I looked pretty innocent at this age. Yet, this is the year I smoked pot.

Fortunately, that same year, my family moved to Utah for my father's work. It happened so suddenly that I was devastated. I had to leave my best friends, knowing that I would not have many opportunities to see them again. We had to leave Seattle behind.

When we arrived in Utah, my world instantly changed. I didn't know anybody, which was awkward at first. My nervousness peaked at recess on the first day of school. I stood watching everyone play a game of football on the playground. I remember hesitating for what seemed like the longest time, before drumming up the courage to finally approach the kids to play. Having some athletic talent helped me to break the ice on the playground. They wanted me on their team. Rather quickly, I adjusted to my new school environment. I eventually made new friends, but it was different than the scene in Seattle. Nobody in my newfound group of friends did drugs. Among this group it was not cool to swear or to shoplift. The kids there were not perfect, but the fun was much more innocent. I never did the crazy things again. I didn't even want to. Moving to Utah really changed my life.

I learned from this experience and others that you become who you hang out with. Environment overrides almost everything in our lives. Where we live impacts us but even more important, it's the people around us and the expectations they have of us that shape who we become. Consequently, choosing wisely who we spend time with may be the single most important priority for our lives.

As Tonya and I have raised our children, that principle has been one of our largest priorities. Our biggest wish for our kids is to be blessed with good friends. This general truth applies to all ages and spectrums of people. Whether we are young or old, married or single, we become like those we choose to spend time with. We often underestimate the impact. I see this effect on myself and others, more and more the older I get.

It is often said, "You are the average of your closest five friends." Current research suggests that isn't completely true. It extends much further than that; it may include people you don't even know. There has been a major study by Nicholas Christakis and James Fowler in which they analyzed the data from the Framingham Heart Study, one of the most robust and longest running health studies ever conducted. They realized they could glean much more than heart health from the participants. They examined the effects that family members and friends had on obesity. They discovered that if our friend had become obese, we were 45% more likely to gain weight in the next 24 to 48 months. What is even more alarming is if a friend of one of our close friends becomes obese our own chances of becoming obese increase 20%. According to the research, this occurs even if we don't personally know the friend of our friend. It continues on, if the friend of the friend of your friend becomes obese you are 10% more likely to become obese.

So our friends influence us, but so do the friends of our friends, and the friends of their friends. As Christakis and Fowler analyzed the decades of data, they were able to come to some conclusions of the cause and effect. Their most prominent explanation is that we are very affected by the norms. If our friend is obese, and his friend is obese and so on and so on, it becomes the norm. This reshapes our perception to make obesity acceptable. We then adjust with this new perception to become more like them. We become comfortable being obese. It is no longer a problem.

We can apply this research to much more than health. When I was sitting at the base of the evergreen tree, my friend who opened the bag of marijuana and began to smoke, had done it before. His friends had done it before, making him more comfortable. For me, smoking marijuana for the first time became very acceptable in that setting. It was the norm in my neighborhood back in the 70's. I wanted to be normal. I gravitated toward my friends' habits, even though my family taught something very different. Had I continued down that path, I would have been able to smoke marijuana without remorse.

The norm is seen in so many areas. In my company I see a culture of doing the right thing for the client and I find it easy to do the right thing for the client. I see companies whose focus is to make as much money as possible without the need for integrity and I see people go down that path with the culture. I see adults who surround themselves with friends who are all divorced and watch them go from a promising marriage to divorce. I see youth who choose to hang out with those who do drugs because acceptance may come easily in that group; then, however, the newbie eventually becomes a drug addict, like his friends. On the other hand, I have then seen drug addicts, which change their friend group to 100% supportive sober people and dig themselves out of the addiction.

We tend to offer negative examples in describing the importance of friends. But on the positive side, choosing to hang out with people who live by wise values is a major opportunity for leverage. Being intentional in choosing friends is a key to our success. If what becomes the norm are the things we see around us, then becoming friends with great people will influence us to be great. I see this in athletics all the time. While training, I try to always be on the bottom half of the talent pool. I want everyone I am around to be more talented and successful then me, so I can learn from and be inspired by their success.

Currently, I run in a group where everyone has completed multiple marathons. I have run only two. I have a goal to qualify for the Boston Marathon. Most of them have run Boston multiple times. The mountain to climb to get there isn't that big of a deal to them. They can tell me how they trained to get there. They can push me on my runs because it isn't too fast to them. They can run it with me when I qualify. By training with them I will qualify for Boston far sooner than if I were to be running in a group with lesser runners, because I will become part of the norm.

There are things that we can control in this life and things we cannot. We control who we spend time with. I have chosen to focus on this in business settings by becoming friends with financial advisors who are the very best in the industry. In my faith I have chosen mentors who have been an example in service. In my social circles I have stayed away from those who would lead me into wrong paths, instead I have tried to pick those with higher standards than I.

When I was in High School, I enjoyed movies like most young men. In our home we stayed away from R rated movies especially those with sex and nudity. My mother would not tolerate it. One day I walked into a house with a friend where an inappropriate movie was playing. It was the type of movie that showed a lot of skin. My friend Troy and I were there when it was turned on. As I began to see all the nudity I had a guilty feeling come over me because I knew it was against my principles to watch it. But I didn't stand up and leave. The guilt was not enough to overcome the guy in me. So we sat mesmerized by the flesh. I will never forget when my friend Troy finally stood up and said, "I am not going to watch any more of this trash." He walked away and I was left there feeling stupid. I have never forgotten that day. He was a better man that day. He made me a better person. He influenced me to be stronger the next time I was faced with that situation. Henry Ford once said, "My best friend is the one who brings out the best in me."

Thus, as previously mentioned, when I became a father, my greatest wish was for my kids to choose good friends. As I speak to other dads in my business and in our church, we all agree that we cannot think of anything more important than for our young people to seek out those who can uplift, encourage, and influence for good. Tonya and I have made this a central focus in our home. As our four kids have grown up, I can attest to the impact it has made on their lives in being successful people. The people with whom we surround ourselves can really dictate the outcomes of our lives.

Questions to consider: Who do I allow into my life? What do they expect of me? Do I want to become like them?

CHAPTER 2

What I Learned From Grandpa

"Everyone loves a Southern gentleman." —unknown author

I carefully climbed onto my grandfather's custom-made dune buggy, one of his most prized possessions, then quickly sat down and buckled up. I could feel the power thrusting from behind as my grandfather revved the roaring engine. With the engine exposed, the sound was deafening. The burning oil produced an aroma that was any car lover's dream. As I looked at my grandpa in the driver's seat, I was anxious yet excited, waiting for takeoff. My heart began to race when my grandfather looked over at me with a grin, then pulled the clutch. We blasted off and left the dust and debris from the freshly cut wheat field flying through the air. Soon the cloud was far behind us.

As a young boy, I was excited but also scared to death. The dune buggy had individual brakes on each rear wheel. Spinning donuts was easy. When grandpa drove through the fields, he would gain speed during a straightaway, then pull hard on one brake while the other rear wheel would continue propelling. We would do doughnuts until it was nauseating. His dune buggy was always jacked up, loud, and fast for maximum fun. While visiting my grandparents, it was one of my most fun and thrilling memories.

This particular summer, my grandparents had invited me to come stay with them for six weeks without my family. My grandparents lived in Ames, Oklahoma, a small, dusty town with only one stoplight. They built their home on a 385-acre plot of land just outside of town. My grandpa called it a beautiful "gentlemen's farm." It had wild turkeys and quail roaming the land. There were wooded areas, cornfields, ponds, rolling hills and even a community lake close by. While Oklahoma doesn't seem like an enticing travel destination, spending the summer alone with my grandparents was a trip of a lifetime.

Upon my arrival, my grandfather immediately had work for me to do. The main project we worked on that summer was to build a retaining wall on the outer edge of the sidewalk around the backside of his house. While constructing the brick wall, it was important to lay the bricks down in a pattern giving the wall an aesthetically pleasing design. There was one corner spot where he wanted me to lay the bricks in a specific order so it could create a certain pattern. He left me to do it without his help. I took my time placing it perfectly according to the pattern he had suggested. I was so proud of my work and couldn't wait to show my grandpa. I was absolutely thrilled to see the smile that came across his face as he viewed the completed project.

The famous dune buggy on Grandpa Allen's farm.

Grandpa had all sorts of ways to have fun.

I learned a few things over that summer that stuck with me even to this day. One of my grandfather's biggest beliefs was that you work hard and then you play hard. This was a common theme each day as we worked vigorously during the day on a given project. Afterwards, it was time to have fun. We would drive the dune buggy, play a round of golf, go skeet shooting, play with a soccer ball, go frog gigging, and of course we would eat. I ate and ate and ate all summer long. They had a Schwann Man deliver Butter Brickle ice cream by the two gallon bucket. They never told me to stay away from the food. Not only did I go from 70 to 85 pounds in six weeks, but also I had a blast. This fun went on all summer long. Gordon B. Hinckley once said, "In all of living, have much fun and laughter. Life is to be enjoyed, not just endured." My grandparents did not just endure life. They loved life. They knew it required both hard work and fun to squeeze the most out of it.

When we look back on our lives, the most prominent memories are usually moments of significance. We forget most of the normal and mundane parts of the day. We often remember some of the best times and the worst times. So it is important to have fun, to create moments of play and laughter to cherish. We never know how long we have. So, those who say we shouldn't wait to have fun in life are wise. It's of high value to make moments to remember now.

After returning home from my grandparent's six-week vacation, I went back to my normal life. Later that October while I was at school, I received a call from the Principal to leave school and go home. I was confused. As I walked into the house, all I could think of was, "What could possibly be a reason to send me home from school? My parents were waiting in the living room to tell me the news. As I entered the room, I knew it must be bad because they had been crying. "Your grandfather has died. He went out on a morning jog and suffered a major heart attack 100 yards from his house. Grandma found him dead off the side of the dirt road in the sagebrush." As I heard the news my heart sank. I cried like a baby.

I received a letter in the mail the next day. My grandfather had written it a couple days prior to his death. He sent me a letter reporting on all the summer activities and projects we had been working on this past summer. He also teased me about the Seattle Seahawks which he enjoyed calling the "Ho Ho Boys." They were not playing so well which was common during that era. How ironic the letter showed up the day after his death. I cherish the letter knowing that he really loved and cared for me. How lucky was I to have my grandparents ask me to spend time with them that summer? Without it, I would have never created all those memories with my grandfather.

Years later when I returned to Oklahoma, I made time to drop by my Grandparents farm. As I went to the spot of my summer brick project, I was taken aback. To my surprise the design was completely asymmetrical. My attempt to make a straight line completely failed. I found it interesting that despite the wall's obvious imperfection, my grandfather allowed me to cement the bricks in the wall and cure it, in order to remember my efforts. I had always thought I had done such a good job, since he had complimented me so much at the time. It meant even more to me when I realized that our experience together was more important to him than perfection.

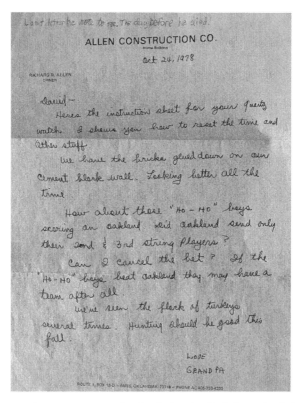

The letter my grandpa wrote to me the day before he died. It arrived three days later.

My grandfather was a great success story. He worked most of his life for the oil company Schlumberger and eventually became one of the top accountants there. After a long stint in Houston, Texas, he eventually left the company in his early 50s. He left his successful career as an executive because they wanted him to relocate to New York City. He was a Texan who didn't want to leave the south, so he resigned and pursued real estate. He then cashed in on a few big deals and retired in his mid 50's. The world would view my grandfather as an accomplished man. When I think of him, I think of a fun, successful, southern gentleman. I was once in a business meeting where four attributes were mentioned that personified a successful person. It spoke to the essence of my grandfather. He lived these throughout his life. It is part of why I admire him so much to this day. When I think of these qualities, I think of him.

Say 'Please' and 'Thank You'

The first of those four attributes is the importance of saying "please" and "thank you." Please and thank you go hand in hand. When you say "please" and "thank you" regularly, people view you differently. It is one way in which we display humility and confidence while showing respect for the person. It is a great way to be polite. Richard Branson once said, "Please be polite. Nothing in life should erode the habit of saying thank you to people or praising them."

My grandparents were preachers of being polite. They taught me table manners the summer I spent with them. It was very important at the table to always say "please" and "thank you" when passing the food. It came from their southern roots. You just did this. They often wouldn't pass the food unless the words were used.

Richard and Geraldine Allen the year they got married.

I rediscovered this principle later in life while attending a monthly small group business meeting where we received constructive criticism and advice to improve our businesses. I received feedback that month that I didn't seem to be a very thankful person. Initially that surprised me. I always felt I was a very thankful person. Then it hit me that most of the time I felt thankful, but had not been intentional in expressing the gratitude I felt. I didn't say "thank you" enough or in the right way. What a shame to feel a certain way and not show it. G.B. Stern said, "Silent gratitude isn't much use to anyone."

Here are some of the best ways I have observed to show thanks. First, look people in the eye and immediately say "thank you" whenever you see the opportunity. That's important, it just makes people feel good. Their task becomes worthwhile to them because they feel recognized and appreciated. Think of the last time you said "thanks" and you saw the recipient just break out in a huge smile. You just made their day. I know my wife feels that way when at the end of dinner we tell her how great it tastes. It puts a smile on her face.

But saying "thank you" should just be the baseline. What I have seen to have the greatest impact is writing a personal note. This seems to be almost a lost art today. In my late twenties, I was the executive secretary to an important leader at my church. At times, I felt way over my head in that position. He mentored me in many ways to help me learn and grow in that role. I remember one day getting a handwritten note in the mail. The note started off by saying, "I was thinking about how much you helped me today and I didn't want that thought to go to waste. So I wanted to reach out and say thanks." It just blew me away. This successful man of prominence was thinking of me and took the time to write me a thank you note. I felt important to him. It meant so much more coming in a note than if he were to have just told me that the next time we were together. I will never forget that letter. It taught me how to inspire and lead people.

Today, I have observed, if someone ever writes a thank you, it most often comes in a text or email. Though that is nice, it has the same effect as verbally saying "Thank you." It doesn't evoke the same emotion as a personal handwritten note. It is partly because of the time and attention the person is taking to write the note. Plus, when it shows up in the mail it comes as a nice surprise for the day. My grandpa's handwritten note surprised me. I have kept it for 41 years. What an example he was. I find if I want to make an impression as a leader or in the business world, one of my greatest tools is a handwritten note.

Show Up On Time

Another of the four attributes of success that my grandfather exemplified was to show up on time. I clearly remember a time in my life when I learned that lesson in an embarrassing way. While I was in grade school my mother introduced me to the piano. She had played most of her life and could perform almost anything. As a child she had taken years of lessons to improve her skills. As the only talented musician in our family, her music filled the house, especially around the holidays.

She started lessons for me at a young age because she wanted me to have music in my life as well. In the beginning I was taught some basic songs. Then I moved on to some classical pieces. I remember thinking those songs were boring. I did learn to play the "Happy Days" theme song. That was cool to me. But most of the songs were not too interesting. I found myself bored with it and would rather be playing with my friends. I didn't enjoy practice and above all I disliked going to piano lessons.

One day, my mom called me into the house because it was time to leave for lessons. I had been playing with my friends and I was not happy to stop so that I could go to practice piano. I complained enough to get my mom a little tense. She wanted to be on time because the teacher required us to be punctual. She hurried me out the door and we headed over to the teachers home. I complained more and more on the drive. It had to be a fun experience for my mom. We finally got there; I stubbornly lay down on the floor of the back seat and wouldn't go inside. My mom got more upset by the minute because we were now late and the teacher would not like it. As I lay there posturing I felt if I were strong enough maybe my mom wouldn't make me go. Then a knock came on the back window. To my horror it was my teacher standing there looking at me curled up on the floor. She had come outside because she could tell something was up. With my head hung low, I opened the door. She said, "David, it is time to come inside, you are late." I was so embarrassed having acted like a baby. I walked inside and had my lesson. Victory for my mother.

I was never late again. I continued to play for two more years, complaining the whole time. My release from piano lessons came when we moved to Utah. I purposely never mentioned to my mother anything about piano or finding a new teacher, and she gave up the battle. She remained the only musician in the family.

I learned from this a lesson how being late can cause some awkward situations for all involved. Typically it affects more than just the one who is tardy. In this case it frustrated both my mother and teacher. That is often the case, which is why we should be on time as regularly as possible.

I'm currently in a running group of four to seven people. One of the reasons I enjoy running with them is everyone shows up on time. If I get the text that we are going to run at 8am, we are running by 8am. I typically get there around 7:50 so that I can walk a bit to warm my legs up. After I stretch a small amount, I am ready to go. If I showed up right at 8am I would not be prepared. I would have to ask if everyone could wait for just a minute. My friends would probably do it but now everyone would be annoyed. If they weren't annoyed, we would eventually always start late.

To me, showing up on time means showing up at least 5 minutes early. This allows us to be prepared to start the meeting, the task, or the event at the selected time. The goal should not be merely to get into the room before the start time. It should mean that we are settled and ready to begin at the start time. If we are ready to go, we are honoring the people we are meeting with. Lik Hock Yap Ivan once said, "If you're early, you're on time. If you're on time, you're late."

Showing up on time is a choice. I have often heard people say, "I just can't make it on time." They are consistently about 5 to 10 minutes late. What is interesting is that for certain events they show up early. I have seen that with our family with church. Most of the family seems to not care if we are late. But for a school choir concert we show up 10 minutes early because we want a good seat front and center. This is a priority; therefore we choose to be on time. I believe we can make the choice to be on time all the time. My grandpa believed that you could.

Do What You Say You Are Going To Do

A third attribute of success I learned from my family and saw exemplified in my grandfather is that we should do what we say we are going to do. This is a principle I came to value in my youth through the dynamics of neighborhood interactions, some healthy and some not so healthy, as you will see.

While living in Washington, my friends and I followed Scott, the leader of the neighborhood. He was three years older than me and was very mature as a middle schooler. He was cool in every way. We all looked up to him. He was superior at nearly every sport we played. He wore the popular Adidas Superstars and had the groovy 70's flared out jeans. He had long light brown wavy hair parted down the middle and hung over his ears. We put him in the same category as the Fonz or John Travolta.

I remember hanging out in his bedroom and looking at all the posters on his wall. I particularly noticed the famous Farrah Fawcett poster hanging next to his bed. We all sat and were mesmerized by her look. We couldn't get her out of our heads. Of course, my mother would have never allowed it in my room. But Scott was cool and had it right where he wanted it.

What was great about Scott, was he accepted the little guy like me even though he was older and cooler. We spent much of our time roaming around the neighborhood finding ways to entertain ourselves. Much of our time was spent playing games and sports of many kinds. Creativity seemed to be our mantra when it came to having fun.

One day while riding our bikes, we decided to build a jump. We got a long piece of plywood and a few bricks from behind our house. When we laid the board down on the bricks it wasn't completely sturdy but was good enough to create a nice ramp. We hoped that the bricks would hold to avoid a disaster.

We started pedaling a few yards away to get the right amount of speed. Too much speed would mean a risk of too much air and possibly an out of control landing. Not enough speed would mean a problem with the takeoff.

When we heard the thrilling sound of the wheels hitting the plywood before the launch we knew we would soon be airborne. We all went off the jump multiple times and had a great time seeing what kind of distance we could get on the landing. No casualties so far.

Scott then came up with a brilliant idea. He said, "I want you guys to lay down just behind the jump and let's see how many people I can jump over." I thought, "Huh, that could really hurt if he landed on me." Luckily my friend Aaron was picked to lay down first. As Scott went off the jump he easily cleared Aaron. We all looked in amazement. He had landed with room to spare.

Unfortunately, it didn't stop there. Scott then said, "I can definitely jump more than one person. So another friend hopped down there and the same thing happened. Scott cleared the two of them with ease. A big grin was on his face. He was having fun now. We, of course, were gaining more respect by the minute. Then he asked for a third person and a fourth. Each time the anxiety got higher and higher. Each time he made it and we thought it was such an impressive feat. Then he looked at me. He said, "Dave, do you want to go next?" In my mind I was thinking, "He hadn't cleared the last guy by very much. If his back wheel lands on my stomach that will really hurt."

Scott could sense my worry. He came up to me and said, "I got this Dave. I will ride even faster to get my furthest distance yet." Coming from Scott, I knew he would do what he said he was going to do. I felt at that moment I could have faith in him.

I went over and lay next to my four young friends lying behind the jump. Even though I had faith, my worries persisted as I lay there looking up into the sky. In my mind I thought again, "It sure seems like a long leap to get over five bodies." I felt very nervous and helpless. We looked at each other with our eyes wide open not really saying much.

My nerves begin to take over as I heard the pedals turn the crank. Scott was accelerating towards us. As he got closer and closer my anxiety grew and grew. "What is about to happen? Will there be any blood?" Then I heard the wheels hit the plywood ramp. In an instant, I saw the RedLine bike soar over the top of us like Evil Knievel jumping over a bus. It happened fast but I quickly learned that he cleared all five of us. My guts were still intact. They were not lying on the street. What relief. What a moment. I could only imagine what my mother would have thought had she peeped out the front window to see the scene unfold before her eyes. It would have made a good home movie.

This neighborhood moment, in our view, only enlarged in our minds the stature of Scott. He was our leader. We followed him into whatever fun he had in mind for the day. Whether it was jumping over us on a bike or beating us in basketball. When Scott said he was going to do it, he did it. Because of this, he impressed us. We wanted to be around him. We wanted to be like him. Scott taught me at a young age how to be respected by others and how to a lead.

Scott and my brother Mike are taking a break from basketball. Scott was the neighborhood leader and seemed cool in every way. We all looked up to him and followed his every move.

If you want to be successful in life, people need to have faith in you. This is essential in your career, in your marriage, and in how your kids perceive you. Being reliable is the way to gain in favor with others. When you do what you say you are going to do once, it is a start. But when you have done it multiple times with consistency you will thrive because people will have faith in you. The dictionary describes reliability as "To be able to produce good results time after time. How much a person can be depended on." When your character personifies reliability, it will take you to heights you could not achieve in life any other way.

We will never be perfect in our reliability and will make mistakes in our journey. That is ok. We can learn from it. I believe if we set a goal to do what we say we are going to do, then start doing it one commitment at a time, over time it will become part of our character.

When I was in 3rd grade my teacher spent a specific day instructing us on what to do when a stranger talks to you. We practiced and role-played much of the day. What stuck out most in my mind was to run away. She then committed us to do this if the occasion ever arose.

That year the instruction was put to the test. I had asked my mom if I could get some candy from the grocery store. She allowed me to walk there by myself. The store was about a half-mile walk from my house. The route left my neighborhood and entered a busy street that had a bunch of storefronts along the road. I had reached the exit of the community and was about to turn on the sidewalk toward the store.

At that point a baby blue 70's Nova drove up beside me. The driver came to a stop and reached to the passenger side to open the passenger door. I had never met him before. The Asian man in his mid 30's looked well kept and normal. He patted on the long vinyl front seat motioning to me and said, "Hop on in, I will give you a ride?" The first thought that came to my mind was "this is not normal." I don't know this guy. Why does he want to give me a ride? I said, "No, I am good. I am just going to the store down the road." Well, he didn't stop there. He patted on the seat again and said, "It's ok, let me give you a ride. Here sit right here." I still remember looking at the front seat and pondering if I should. The thought of the teacher came into my head. I should do what she told us to do. So I got the courage to tell him "No" again.

I was about to run when he asked me again. Looking back, what really scares me was he asked a third time. Why? What is the reason he would want me to get in the car so badly? I looked at him nervously and cautiously and said, "No" one last time. He gave up and closed the door and drove away. Immediately the thought came to me. "You are supposed to run. So I took off running as fast as I could. Although I ran, I did run towards the grocery store versus home because I hadn't bought my candy yet.

Doing what I said I would do in that situation saved my life. Looking back, I can't think of a reason why this man would have ever done this except for an evil purpose. What a horrible story this could have turned out to be. How sad it would have been for my parents. In this instance, I did what I was taught. I followed through on my commitment to my teacher when it mattered most. It is one of my most important accomplishments in my life.

Finish What You Started

Dan Gable, the wrestling coach for the Iowa Hawkeyes in the 70's and 80's, illustrated a fourth attribute of success I saw in my grandfather. He coached his team to 16 national championships during his tenure there. He may have been one of the greatest coaches of any sport ever. He certainly would have been on the Mt. Rushmore of coaching legends with John Wooden, Bill Belichick, and others. He had a motto that he instilled upon his wrestlers, "Always finish on top." As a wrestler himself, he only lost one match his entire collegiate career. He was always in the lead. One reason for his success is he would never let up till the clock hit zero. He always finished on top of the other wrestler, not underneath him, where his opponent could get a point or two. He felt if you were just trying to run out the clock, you risk having bad things happen. His teams internalized this and dominated for more than a decade.

I think so much in life is about the finish. We have to finish what we start. I tell my kids I'm not going to make you try out for that sport or music lesson or whatever, but when you start you are going to finish it. When we follow through with things it is where we truly learn the most.

Most of the time when we start something we assume we can learn to do it well. Invariably, when we are learning an instrument or playing a sport, there will be difficult moments. Sometimes it takes us to the brink and we just want to give up. The famous boxer Mike Tyson once said, "Everyone thinks they have a plan, until I punch them in the face." Most things worthwhile in life are an upward climb. It is undoubtedly going to get hard. We will get punched in the mouth a few times. We should expect that and resolve to find solutions to work through it.

I remember in grade school having an interest in art. My grandmother was an oil painter and had beautiful paintings all over the walls of her home. We had a couple of her paintings in ours as well. I would look at them and dream that I could do that. I tried to paint using watercolor as well as oil paint. Nothing that I did was really that impressive. My mother would praise me to build my self-esteem, but my art looked very much like it came from an elementary student.

I got pretty discouraged and could have given up. But, one day I looked at a cartoon. I noticed that the cartoons told a story. I thought that I should try that. I developed a thought around my family. I called it "The Peaceful Family of the Shuley's." I figured it would be fun to show our whole family going at each other. Even though we had a peaceful home in general. I thought it would be fun to poke fun.

The technique I used was to look at other cartoons in the newspaper and see the nose of one character that could look like my dad's nose; then I would draw it as closely as I could on my drawing. I would take the eyes of another random character from the newspaper that looked like my dad's eyes and draw them as closely as I could.

I was not talented enough to simply draw a cartoon face and have it resemble someone. Looking at other cartoons gave me a method that worked. I was able to draw each character that way. It captured my whole family in an interesting chaotic moment that actually looked like them. I was able to do something impressive that showed ability above that of my age. Even though I was discouraged at first, I had found a way to make it work.

To this day, my mother has the 4th grade framed cartoon on her wall. I have since drawn many cartoons using the same method. They have been nice gifts for my friends and family through the years.

A cartoon I drew of my family while in 4ᵗʰ grade. A therapist could have fun interpreting my psyche from what is going on in the picture. Luckily child services weren't called. What's funny is my memory of this portion of my childhood was a happy, safe home.

I believe that this principle of finishing what we start should be learned at a young age and continually practiced, as we grow older. Angela Duckworth wrote in her book titled "Grit" that the most successful athletes, musicians, artists, executives and business owners have found a passion and have the capacity to keep at it for years and years. They possess grit. There is something internally developed within them to work through difficult things. When the difficulties come, they do not see the hardships as unfair. They view them as obstacles that eventually can be overcome. They realize they simply need to find a way to do it. She said, "Never quit on any activity when things are going bad. Only quit while it is going well and you have a clear mind to know that it is no longer an interest of yours." Most of us do the opposite. We quit once it gets hard and messy. Not because we lack interest in the subject, but that it is too hard.

Angela also believes that the path to success often involves trying many things along the way to discover one's talents and interests. These interests may change over time and we may not be very successful with some, but we have the benefit of learning something from each new discipline.

One summer day I wanted to make some money. Most kids would think that opening a lemonade stand would be the best way. I had a different idea. I was so excited. I didn't tell anyone about my plans, not even my parents. After I found the supplies I needed, I placed a chair and a table on the lawn in front of our house. Then I put the comb, scissors, and water bottle on the table. Next, I drew on a poster board with a dark marker, "Haircuts for a Dollar." I sat there with such excitement and confidence that this could be a really big deal. As I sat out in front of my house for some reason no one came. This seven-year-old barber had no customers. I sat and sat for what seemed like hours, but no customers. I couldn't figure out why people didn't want to get a haircut from me. After a while, with my head held low, I packed up my supplies and called it quits.

Some ideas are simply not very good or viable. Some things we should quit doing. In the streets of my neighborhood, I never became the famous child barber. There was a good reason for that. Angela Duckworth suggested that even gritty people are not supposed to continue indefinitely every passionate idea. Some things are just not a fit. She found in studies that when children attempt an activity like soccer, as an example, if they initially enjoy it and are excited about it, they should stay with it for more than one season before deciding to move on. If they quit after just one season they may not have had time for any obstacles to work through. Two seasons or more they will have gone through the challenges and are in a better situation to comprehend if it is a fit or not. Colleges look for extracurricular activities on applications, partly because it is an indicator of future success. They feel if you were able to overcome initial problems and succeed in those activities, you will more likely be able to finish what you start while in college.

One example from my life when I encountered initial setbacks but persevered to succeed, was my experience with the Boy Scouts. Our church used the scouts for part of its youth program. I was not a natural scout like my older brother. He loved to buy fishing and camping gear and to get dirty in the wilderness. At that age, I preferred athletics and the indoors.

One particular campout sticks out to me. We were in the middle of the Uinta Mountains of Utah. This is true wilderness. No campgrounds or services were close by to make life easy. It was just the natural beauty of the outdoors. Our goal as scouts was to reach camp as soon as possible. The 5-mile hike would normally be beautiful and fun. But this day it was pouring rain with chilly temperatures. We could barely see the trail in front of us. We each carried a backpack that became a nuisance almost from the start. My mom had purchased for me a cheap version that never seemed to distribute the weight to my hips. It was always slipping and caused my shoulders to bear the burden.

In the pouring rain a few of us decided to walk ahead of the adults to get to our destination by the lake as quickly as possible. We miserably slogged through the cold rain at a quick pace. We soon found ourselves way ahead of the troop. It was only five of us that had chosen to go this fast. We arrived at the lake and quickly realized that it wasn't any warmer once we were there. In fact we got even colder waiting for everyone else to arrive.

We came up with an idea. Let's build a fire to get warm. Because of the rain coming down we couldn't find a place of shelter unless we stood underneath the large trees in the area. We built the fire right at the base of a large Douglas fir tree. In our minds it was a perfect plan. We could stay dry and warm ourselves. Well, we started the fire and began to warm up. My hands began to get a feeling in them again. It was heaven all the way up until my scout leader showed up. He could not believe we would consider lighting a fire at the base of a tree. He gave us a tongue-lashing. He was irate. The fire had scarred the base black to about 3 feet off the ground. Who knows if we could have eventually burned the whole thing down? Starting a fire in that way was clearly not part of the scout handbook and he let us know it.

All I remember about that day is I wanted to be home. I wanted my warm house. I knew I was missing some socially fun activity at the school that night. I just wished I could be anywhere but on this cold wet mountain. The thought continued through my mind, "Scouting sucks."

Well, my scouting career did not end there. I went on many more camp outs, river trips, hiking exhibitions, cave explorations, and so forth. I learned to enjoy many parts of it. It ended up being a part of my life that created many adventures and good memories with my friends. I was in scouting for over four years. It taught me how to achieve goals. I was the first person in my congregation to achieve the Eagle Scout Award. I completed the requirements before the age of 14. It helped me learn how to do something hard and overcome some difficult challenges along the way. It gave me some grit while giving me the good feeling that I finished what I started. As I look back on it, I am so glad I stuck it out and did not quit because of a few bad initial experiences.

A question to consider: Which of these four principles do I lack in my daily living?

1. **Say "Please and Thank you."**

2. **Show up on time.**

3. **Do what you say you are going to do.**

4. **Finish what you started.**

CHAPTER 3

How We Process The Environment Around Us

"No pessimist ever discovered the secret of the stars, or sailed to an uncharted land, or opened a new heaven to the human spirit." –Helen Keller

My legs were exhausted. They were pounded by the last four miles of downhill. The sweat dripping down my legs had become dried, crystallized, white stains from the miles and miles of running. The sun bearing down from above made the taste of Gatorade a dream. There were no crowds cheering at this stage of the race. It was just the sounds of the runner's shoes hitting the payment. As I looked at the long road ahead with nothing but desert sagebrush and red rock around me, I said to myself, "Just keep going, you can make it."

I had run 16 miles before, but knowing I still had 10 miles left was a daunting thought. Being twelve years old, I was used to my parents instructing me on things, but today I was alone with no one there to help. So much of running a marathon is mental. For me, I was tired and naive but I assumed I would somehow make it. My mind stayed away from bad places.

By mile 18, I had two problems. One, I felt extremely tired. Second, I needed to use the bathroom. At this point of the race both are not good. To help with the first, I allowed myself to walk for the first time. This would hurt my time, but I didn't care. I didn't plan on walking long.

As people jogged by they said words of encouragement. They

probably felt sympathy for such a young kid at this stage of the race. I kept telling them, "I am good."

The only problem with walking was it increased my need to poop. Almost like a baby dropping before birth, it was ready to come out. My body began to have tingling sensations, which caused a slight panic. I didn't have much time. There were no porta potties anywhere in sight. All I could see was sagebrush for miles ahead. I had to make an executive decision.

I decided it was time to go for it. I walked about 30 feet off the road into the desert field. I looked for the largest sagebrush I could find. Unfortunately, there wasn't any large one to hide behind, so I just picked the fullest one. Being committed now I pulled down my shorts and squatted to do my business. What an awkward relief. Runners just ran by me with zero curiosity. Marathons have a way of eliminating discretion.

After my stop, I was a new young man. I got back on the road and started running again. I felt a second wind and gained confidence in every step that I would make it to the finish. I got within 6 miles of the finish, then 3, and then 1. At that point, I could see the finish down the long straight away. As I crossed the line the crowds were cheering along with my family. What a relief. What an accomplishment!

I went and lay down in a shaded area of grass. I felt total exhaustion yet total happiness that I finished. I was proud of myself because a 3:56 minute marathon was a decent time for my age group. Just finishing a marathon at my age was a huge deal. I took 5th in my age division, which was eligible for a trophy. To this day, it is my most prized trophy.

Running in my life started on a Friday night at Godfather's Pizza. My family was there with friends from the neighborhood. My dad had started running with them that week and they chatted about their recent jogs. As I sat there with interest I learned about what they were doing. My father sensed this and the following morning he asked if I wanted to run with him. I jumped on the idea.

It was a sunny warm Saturday morning for an early March in Utah. He wanted to go five miles. We headed out for my first run ever. I enjoyed being with my dad one on one in this way. We talked and had a good time. We had to stop a couple times to get through it, but by the end I had worked out and really enjoyed my time with dad.

He asked me if I wanted to run with the other men of the neighborhood. It sounded fun, so the next week my dad and I woke up early before school to head out the door. When we met the other men, they were extra nice and included me in the group. I felt really cool being around all of these older men. As we ran, I heard all the stories from their adult lives. I found it fun to get to know them in this way. I didn't have to say much; I just needed to stay up with them. It wasn't a problem.

After running for a couple months the group decided to train for the St. George Marathon. The race was in the fall where we would have 5 months to train. It sounded far but if they could do it, I thought I could.

We trained all summer. The long runs were fun. Many times other runners would jog by and ask how far we were going. One day, I remember telling them 18 miles and they just looked at me as if I were lying. I smiled.

Unfortunately, my dad broke his leg three weeks before the marathon. He was running early in the morning when it was still dark. He planted his foot where the edge of the road dropped off to a dirt path. When he went down hard his leg snapped. He was very disappointed. He was in great shape. When the day of the race came, he had to watch us run without him.

Much of my running experience was because of my dad. I would have never started running nor ever completed a marathon at such a young age without his influence. He asked me to run that first day. I enjoyed having conversations with dad on those long runs through the neighborhoods.

My dad and I were close. I looked up to him. He came to all my sporting events. He spent time with us even though he was working hard in the life insurance business making a living. He taught us how to laugh and work. Many times on Labor Day he told us that we had to join him to work in the yard. He said, "Why else would they call it Labor Day." He was always there for dinner to lead the conversation. He and my mother gave us security that could come in no other way.

The finish of the 1981 St. George Marathon.

About 3 weeks after the marathon my dad asked to have all the kids come into the kitchen. My brother (age 15), my sister (age 10) and I sat down at the table and he looked at us in a somber manner then said, "I want you kids to know that I love you. I care about you very much. What I am about to tell you does not change that. Your mother and I are splitting up. I don't love her the same anymore. I am moving about an hour away to Provo, Utah and will be living in a motel. Your mother will stay here with you. I will visit every couple weeks on the weekends. I am sorry. This must be hard for you."

As a young boy I didn't know what to think. Tears welled up in my eyes instantly. My mind was racing. My parents never fought in front of us. They seemed like normal parents. We did everything together. How could this be? How could dad be saying this? What does this mean? How will my life be different? Question after question raced through my mind. But all I could do is just sit there in silence.

Dad left that day. He was gone. All of the daily runs were over. All the family dinners, family trips, the financial security, the happy times. They were over. There was a new reality. The new reality was uncertainty. Why did he go? Can we stay in the house? Mom looks terribly sad, how will she take care of us? Will they get a divorce? Will we be able to stay in the same school? What do I say to dad the next time I see him? What will I tell my middle school friends? This began the hardest period of my life.

My dad, brother, and I playing in the snow. I must have lost.

Family photo when my parents were separated. How could my mother have bought me that baby blue suit? Stylish.

A month later I was in gym class, my best friend said to me, "I heard your M and D are separated." I straight up lied to him and said they were not. I was embarrassed and upset. Life was a bit out of my control, it was new, it was uncertain, I didn't know how to deal with it and I didn't like it. I was sad and upset and I let it get to me.

I remember seeing my dad for the first time at the temporary motel where he was staying. I hated that motel. I wondered what was going on in there. I had a dark feeling every time I saw the sign in front. Everything was so different. That motel represented pain. Years later, when I drove by the place that familiar pain came right back.

There are so many things in life that are out of our control. When bad things occur in this way, it can be very difficult. As humans we are hardwired to want to have control of our environment. But we can't control everything. I had no way to keep my dad from leaving that day.

What helps me is to control what I can control. It all starts with my attitude. I was a naturally happy person. Most days were good for me. So when I had family issues the happy disposition was put to the test. I found that my attitude made the difference.

Chuck Swindoll once said, "The longer I live the more I realize the effect of attitude on my life. Attitude, to me, is more important than facts. It is more important than the past, than education, than money, than circumstances, than successes, than what other people think or say or do. It will make or break a company, a church or a home. The remarkable thing is we have a choice every day regarding the attitude we will embrace for the day. We cannot change the past... we cannot change that people will act in a certain way. We can do nothing to change the inevitable. The only thing we can do is play on the one string we have, and that is our attitude. I am convinced that life is ten percent what happens to me and ninety percent how I react to it. And so it is with you...We are in charge of our attitudes!"

I have known people who always seem happy and I have known those who always seem unhappy. It's tempting to think that their attitude is primarily a result of their circumstances, but I believe it is more about how they view their circumstances. Shawn Achor, the author of "The Happiness Factor," states that 90% of our happiness is based on how we process the environment around us.

A helpful practice for me is to always start my prayers with three things for which I am thankful. The three things have to be specific to that day. I can't say the same as I did the day before. Shawn Achor discovered that stating daily three things we are thankful for has proven to be a key step to create happiness within us.

Our attitudes affect how we see the world. Our focus determines our reality. When I feel like things are off-balance for me, I try to remember to ask myself if I am focusing on the positive or negative? I want to be intentional about directing my life in a positive direction. This is not a small thing.

Being intentional on how we process the environment around us is so helpful when working through difficulty. Am I going to view things positively or negatively? I have always tried to be a "cup half full" kind of guy versus a "cup half empty."

Trevor Moawad has researched this subject matter for years. He has consulted numerous athletes in the top of their fields. His study indicates that positive thinking only increases effectiveness by 3% to 5%. In the example of an athlete, his or her talent does the large majority of the work. Positive thinking simply steers the ship.

But negative thinking is proven to have large impact on one's life. Trevor states that negativity can slow or dampen creativity by 18% and increase unintentional errors by 30%. According to this study, negative thinking, then, is four to seven times more powerful than its equivalent: positive thinking. In similar studies, Mao and Cleveland clinics have established that 83% of illnesses are facilitated, acerbated, or started from negative thinking.

An additional element in Moawad's research regards the consumption of negative information. He states that watching 3 minutes of negative news increases by 27% the chance that we will think we have had a terrible day. This illustrates the panic the internet can create in our lives. What we consume matters.

Having said this, it is important to remember that everyone has negative thoughts. There is nothing wrong with us or unnatural when we have them. Even the most successful athletes, the greatest leaders, and the top performers have negative thoughts fairly frequently. Our bodies, for thousands of years, have needed the negative hardwiring to protect us and keep us safe. Fear and pain can be a healthy element to being aware of and prepared for the challenges around us.

What we need to guard against most, however, is verbalizing the negative. Moawad's studies show that if we say our negative thoughts out loud, the impact is 10 times more powerful than if we just think them. "I am not smart enough." "I am always sick." "This is too hard for me to ever accomplish." It turns out that saying negative things out loud increases 40 to 70 times the probability of what we don't want to happen to actually happen. This is of enormous consequence.

So what do we do about it? Moawad says that for starters we can do something simple. STOP SAYING OUTLOUD OUR NEGATIVE THOUGHTS. How we talk about negativity is something we, personally, can control. Saying nothing will give our brains the best functionality going forward. This will greatly affect our performance and mindset in whatever difficulty we are trying to overcome.

Regarding our persistent negative thoughts, going from negative thinking to positive thinking can be hard. Moawad suggests one first focus on "Neutral Thinking." He says that where "Positive" thinkers screw up is they ignore what is real in their circumstance and hope that repeating positive thoughts will just magically change things. He suggests that we accept the past as real. For example, it may be true that: "We played a bad half," and "This health challenge has been horrible and won't go away," and "I messed up." However, we should keep in mind that while the past is real, it is not predictive. What we do next is what determines our future. Not how we feel. NO FEELING IS FINAL. We need simply to find a way to move forward.

Angela Duckworth stated regarding this, "Optimists habitually search for temporary and specific causes for their suffering." She explains that they have a mindset that they have the capacity to figure out a way to work through problems and overcome them. They just have to find a way.

Pessimists, on the other hand, "assume permanent and pervasive causes are to blame." Pessimists feel like there is nothing they can do about it. The problem is fixed and out of anyone's control.

Angela cited a test developed to distinguish optimists from pessimists: Imagine at your employment—"You can't get all the work done that others expect of you. Now, imagine one major cause for why this happened. What leaps into your mind?" After you read this hypothetical scenario, write down your response.

She continues, "If you are a pessimist, you might say, "I screwed up everything." Or, "I am a loser." These inner narratives seem to be deeply embedded in the psyche of a pessimist. It's very difficult to change them. They're also pervasive; they're likely to influence a lot of life situations, not just one's job performance. Permanent and pervasive explanations for adversity turn minor complications into major catastrophes. They make it seem logical to give up. If, on the other hand, you are an optimist, you might say, "I mismanaged my time." Or "I didn't work efficiently because of distractions." "These explanations are all temporary and specific; their fix-ability motivates you to start clearing them away as problems."

I agree with Angela Duckworth's research. I found that with my dad's leaving, I had a tough change in my life. But I got to choose how I thought about the change. I remember the day everything began to change. A month or two after my dad moved out, he took me skiing. It was one of those sunny warm days on the slopes. We were not the best skiers but good enough to ski together on the green runs. It was the first time I had been one on one with my dad since the split. It was a great day. We had a lot of fun together on the sunny slopes. I sat on the lift that day and found myself having a conversation with him. It wasn't that deep. We weren't solving all the problems that surrounded us. We were just having a good time. At one point while riding up the lift I said to myself, "I sure have fun with my dad. It is so nice to be with him." It was a good thought. I hadn't thought about that for a while. What happened next was wonderful. At that moment some of the anger dissipated. I decided I would focus from now on to just enjoy being around my dad when I had the chance to be with him. I would do my best to stop thinking about the negative thoughts of the situation. I couldn't control what happened with my parents but I could love him and have fun with him. That was what I could control.

My attitude completely changed from anger and confusion to looking forward to spending time with my dad. With this changed attitude, I started to become my happy positive self again. Things weren't perfect but I was in a good place. It was all about my attitude.

After about eight months of our parents being separated, eight months of trying to keep the details of my family away from my friends, eight months of watching my mom struggle, eight months of church friends rallying around us, my dad and mom decided to work it out. It was a great day when my dad came home. However, there was a somber tone to the reunion. Damage had been done. It would never totally be the same. There was always the lingering worrisome thought, "Could it happen again?" But we were together. Over time, life settled into a normal cadence. Family life became something to be happy about again. As I look back, I feel very blessed that my parents were together for my upcoming teenage years. I was proud that when they had a problem, they didn't abandon each other but worked on it enough to get back together.

Heading out on the slopes with my dad.

Some Things Are Just Sad

A couple years later I was in the 8th grade in middle school. I was in the Boy Scouts with many of my friends. Our leader usually picked us up for scouts and we piled into his large beat up van.

One night I was in the van and we went to one of my best friend's houses to pick him up. I stayed in the car with some others as my leader and another friend of mine went to the door. I noticed when they knocked, no one answered. Eventually our leader finally opened the door and walked in. They did not come out for quite some time. I had no idea what they were doing in there. I was starting to get impatient.

What I didn't know is at the very moment my leader knocked on the door, my friend's brother was in his bedroom with a gun to his head. His older sister was begging him to not shoot the gun. My friend was sitting in the other room, paralyzed, as he listened to the conversation between his brother and sister.

His brother had suffered from depression and had for quite some time been on medication. He had done so well with the medication that he decided to go off of it because he didn't feel like he needed it anymore. Well, his depression crashed and he became suicidal.

As he sat in the bedroom with his sister pleading with him to give her the gun he finally shot himself in the head. When the shot went off it was at the very moment my scout leader had walked inside the house. They rushed downstairs to the room to see what happened and began mouth-to-mouth resuscitation and chest compressions. It was to no avail, he died within seconds of the shot. They all sat there bloody, devastated, and traumatized.

We saw them walk out to the van with their heads hanging low and they immediately told us what had happened. We were overwhelmed. Our Scout leader drove us to the church where he then shared the news with our friend's parents. I will never forget watching the father run out of the church through the parking lot to his car holding his hand over his mouth to cover his sorrow.

Later that night I went to my friend's house to take him with another guy to just shoot some basketball at the neighbor's court. We didn't know what to say so we just shot around and tried to be there for him. As a 13-year-old boy I doubt I had much to say of value.

From that night our friendship greatly deepened. I think living through something like that together changes things a bit. Being there for a friend in mourning is one of the most special things we can do for someone. They don't forget it and it bonds people together.

We ended up not only being best friends in high school, but also in college. We ran together on the high school cross-country team. We roomed together at BYU. I even set him up with his future wife during our senior year of college. They were meant for each other. The weekend of graduation from BYU consisted of the graduation ceremony and my friend's wedding where I was one of two best men.

A year after graduation he had moved with his wife to California. Along with some other college friends, I went on a vacation to Las Vegas to see him and have a good time together. It was there that he first asked me the question. He said that in the last year he had noticed he was beginning to hear voices in his head. He had never had this happen before. He had visited a doctor who had suggested some medication would be helpful for this kind of thing. He asked me that day, if I thought he should get on medication. I didn't know much about this area at all but suggested he probably should if the doctor suggested it. He was fearful because of his older brother's negative history with the ups and downs of medication.

I left that trip without thinking too much of it, because he was totally himself. Maybe just a little quieter than normal, but still we had a great time.

The next time I saw him was a year later at my wedding. When I first said hello, I noticed that there was a very different look in his eyes. He had an anxious disposition. He looked almost scared to talk to me. It was my wedding day, and I wasn't able to talk to him much, but something was very different. I told Tonya that something was wrong with my friend.

A year later we came back to visit he and his wife again. At this point his schizophrenia had taken over. I was scared sleeping at his house. He would talk normally for a minute, then blow up screaming F-bombs at me as if I had done something horrible to him. At one point we had gone to the Sundance Ski resort to hike. Afterward, he was driving down the canyon and had an episode. Tonya and I thought he might drive us off a cliff. He was flying down the canyon and yelling at us for saying things about him behind his back (Which we had never done, but the disease told him we were doing so.)

When we left their house, I was devastated. What had become of my friend? Early on he had refused to take medication because of his brother's history. Then, once his disease had progressed, he stood his ground without being open to any input. It is very sad and frustrating, because with today's science, he could be treated for his particular disease. His younger brothers have had the same chemical imbalance and have lived quality normal lives.

It has been 22 years since that trip and my wife and I were only able to see him one more time. It was a brief visit. His wife stayed married to him for 10 years before finally leaving him. He has never allowed me to come visit since. I have texted him numerous times but he always says he is too busy.

My friend was brilliant, funny, athletic, and truly a good, loving person. He was one of my best friends for over 14 years. But due to his disease, he has lived as a hermit in recent decades, all by himself, in a house his parents bought for him. Instead of following his dream to be a college professor, he now has a hard time holding even menial jobs. He still runs a lot but spends most of his life by himself.

This is one of the saddest things I have ever seen. Unfortunately, I have experienced other sad things, such as family divorce, death in the family, alcoholism with people close to me, gambling addictions, and more. These things are just sad and in most cases there isn't a thing I could do more to help the situation. It is just sad. I guess that is one of the lessons of life. There are sad things you have to witness.

My only advice I would give to influence attitude is twofold. They both require a positive outlook. First, never give up on loving the person. My wife has said many times that we can't change people's lives. They have to choose to do it themselves. They have to execute on the change. What we can do is love them. We can be there for them. We can be an example for them. We can share our thoughts with them. But most of all we hope they can remember that we loved and cared for them.

In my life, as I look back on 51 years, there are very few people that have really changed in a major way because of me. The ones that changed came to the realization that they needed to and they did it themselves with support of those around them. The only role I could really play in their lives was to love them and encourage them. I believe that is most important: showing love in any sad situation we might be a part of. We are unique and we can impact with love in our own way that no one else can.

My second piece of advice is to never give up hope in an afterlife. It is so important to believe this. In an afterlife we have the potential for these problems to make sense. In the afterlife illnesses can be erased. In the afterlife love can prevail. In the afterlife we can live with our loved ones and with God. We can see that things can become right in the end. For me, when I have faith in this, I can picture a better day. J.R.R.Tolkien once said, "In sorrow we must go, but not in despair. Behold! We are not bound forever to the circles of the world, and beyond them is more than memory."

This really helps me deal with the sad things of life. I don't view my friend at fault in any way for his mental illness. It is just there, it happened, and it is sad to watch. But I do believe that in the world to come, his mind will be clear and in some way everything will be all right. I will have the capacity to enjoy that relationship again and to watch it grow from there. This belief, this hope, gives me peace and allows me to cope with the sadness that the circumstance brings.

Questions to consider: What lens do I view the world through? Is it positive or negative?

CHAPTER 4

See Your Future

"Believe that nothing is too good to be true." —unknown author

Jennie was the most popular girl at Orem High. As the captain of the varsity cheerleading team, her looks turned everyone's heads. She was a distraction at the many high school sporting events. Not only did she have that long 80's permed hair and a big smile but she was actually a nice person. She spent her time with the quarterback of the football team and any other guy she chose. She was untouchable by most common guys like me. I was a cross-country runner. Enough said. This didn't keep me from dreaming about that possible date someday in the future.

We had moved to Orem, Utah soon after my parents got back together. Time in this new place had been good to me. I developed many new friends during middle school and high school. During one hot summer day with my friends Brian and Nathan, we had nothing to do. Conversation turned to Jennie and that dream date. Nathan said, "Why don't you just ask her out? In fact, let's do it today." Just the thought of it made me nervous.

My mind raced on how I could make a good impression. She knows me but I am not on her radar. How could I stand out? Nathan had in front of his house a row of pink rose bushes. I came up with a plan. We went outside and cut a half dozen roses then wrapped them in newspaper. I figured she would be impressed.

We drove to her home. My nerves grew and grew; the closer we got to her house. I had many thoughts go through my head. What was I going to say? How do I look to her? Would she turn me down? Is this dream going to become a reality? My hands began to get clammy as I pulled up to the house. Is this really going to happen?

I walked up to the front porch. My friends stayed in the car. They loved watching me go through this. As I looked over and saw their smiles and chuckles I said to myself, "They are not helping." I was already nervous enough.

As I stood on the porch I gathered enough courage to ring the doorbell. While I waited, I looked down at the homemade bouquet of flowers. For a moment I was proud of my idea. She will feel so special. But then to my horror, a large centipede appeared from beneath the newspaper. It began crawling up the rose petal. It was so gross. The brown, slimy skin was sure to put a different expression on her face than what was intended. Then the scene got worse, it's twin appeared. I panicked not knowing what to do. I quickly did my best to flick them off not knowing how many more were undiscovered. As I was flicking bugs, the door opened and there stood Jennie.

With sweat beading up on my forehead I extended my arm and gave her the flowers. In my head I was praying that there were no more bugs that would come out. As I stood there like a statue I felt so out of her league. Clearing my throat I asked her if she were able to go on a date this weekend. She was probably surprised by my visit and hesitantly said, "Sure." I bolted before she could change her mind.

The weekend could not come quick enough. I had this dream of Jennie having a great time on the date and starting to like me. It was only a dream. I really didn't ever think it was going to happen. Why would she like a runner when she could have a quarterback?

The date was cordial. She was polite. I found it wild just being in her presence. The thought went through my head; "I am on a date with the most popular and attractive girl in the school." I am sure she could sense my admiration. It was not a turn on. But throughout the night I could see by her body language that this was a one and done. At the end of the evening I said goodnight with a hug and the dream was over. I knew where I stood. I wasn't desperate enough to keep trying. Time to move on.

My high school buddies and I had many adventures together.

I think it is important to dream. With God we have the ability to even dream bigger. I have found that in most things in life I go big. Whether it is my family life, trips we take, houses we build, projects we start, sporting goals we work to achieve, I typically don't like to feel that we are settling for something ordinary.

But one thing I learned in high school is that just dreaming of something doesn't make things happen. I had a dream of Jennie as my girlfriend. That was big. Many considered her as the most coveted date in the school. What was missing was inside my head. I saw myself going on a date but I never saw myself as her boyfriend. I couldn't visualize it. From my point of view, she was in a different universe. I just hoped it would happen. I couldn't see it.

Hoping for things doesn't accomplish much, because typically hoping doesn't include much action, much faith in us or faith in God. Hoping for something is akin to a wish. I have no memory of any of my birthday wishes ever coming true.

In my junior and senior year of high school I was one of the top cross-country runners in the state of Utah. I won many races including some large invitationals and regional meets. I had great confidence in many races and knew that I would win. I just hoped to be state champion. When it came to the state meet, even though I was talented enough, I never saw it happening. I just dreamed of it. I don't know what kept me from that confidence. I just had not developed it yet.

At the actual state meets, I not only didn't win but I died at them. My best finish was 4th which included runners beating me that had never, throughout the season. I didn't show up and was always upset afterward. I look back on it now and realize my biggest problem is I didn't expect to win.

What is the key to faith, the key to dreams, the key to having big things happening? It is to visualize it taking place. Someone I really admire once told me: "See it in your future. Really see it happening. If you expect it to be in your future, it will be just a matter of time." I have found my friend to be correct. When we see, visualize, and plan the steps to something, eventually it is no longer a dream, it becomes a reality. We can later sit back and say to ourselves, "It is amazing how this all unfolded."

There were a few things at a young age I always visualized would happen. I saw myself being a missionary after high school. I saw myself getting married, I saw myself having children. I saw myself being successful in a career.

In the region meet of my junior year I dominated the race.

When I was in my 20's and 30's I saw myself being close to my wife and kids, being in the top 20 for my company, building a dream home, traveling the world, being able to retire in my 50's. All of these things have unfolded. Not always in the timing that I expected but they all eventually took place.

Currently I see myself running the Boston Marathon, serving as a mission president for my church, and having a great impact on young people's lives. I just see it. No one can predict the future. But visualizing it is the key to impacting and shaping the future. It is a key to having faith.

I think an important point to consider is to create dreams that are in line with God's will. Visualization works without involving God. But when we include God in our plans they have a way of getting bigger, more impactful, and meaningful. When our dreams align with His will, we tend to be filled with more joy when we accomplish it. Maybe because His will is to create joy in our lives. If our desires match up, it is a win win.

Having Him behind our dreams gives us even more confidence. It creates more faith and greater capacity to visualize the future. I find when my dream is something I feel God desires for me, I have an easy time seeing it happen. I can then ask for His help. Dreams are never easy, so it is nice to ask for God's help. Joseph Smith once said, "When a man of faith asks the Lord for something, he generally gets it." I have seen that happen frequently throughout my life.

There are three steps to turning dreams into something we see happening. First, I spend time writing down on paper goals for this year. Then, separately I go into my visions of exactly what I want my next three to five years of my life to look like. I am very descriptive in this process. It is in paragraph form. I describe specifically what I want my family, physical, spiritual, financial, and social life to look like. This is actually fun to do.

It is important to keep in mind during this dreaming phase, that anything is possible. I continue to remind myself: Just dream big. If I know it is aligned with God, I can feel free to go for it, not holding back. Some people feel they don't deserve good things to happen. That is head trash. We can accomplish with God so much more than we could ever do on our own.

To align our dreams with God there are few principles that are important to consider. The dreams should be moral and ethical in nature. We should feel that they would be good for our family, our community, and us. Most dreams that help others seem to get extra help from God.

Another principle I want is for my dreams to feel right. We might feel the Holy Spirit bring peace that this dream is aligned with God's word. Or some might just feel it in the gut that it is a good direction. Regardless, it seems wise to pray and reflect first before just deciding on one's goals.

So truly dream and put into writing what the perfect world can look like, describing it in terms of one's ideal social, physical, financial, emotional, spiritual, and relationships. I always tell people, "Go into detail describing your perfect future. Once you know what you want, that is the seed of directing your life."

One of the biggest compliments I have ever received came from a friend in a business study group. He said, "Dave, I have noticed you run your life. You don't let your life run you." I believe it starts with knowing what you want and having it written down where you see it everyday. I have my goals and vision next to my bathroom sink where I see them while shaving.

The second step to seeing dreams turn into reality is to get our minds to believe that these goals will really be achieved. However, sometimes believing it will happen is not easy. At first our dreams seemed like hopes. The best way I have found to change our dreams from something we HOPE for to something we KNOW will happen in our future is a daily mental exercise that I do before bed every night. It can be done first thing in the morning or night before bed, but it's wise to make it the same time each day. I got my mental exercise technique from author Jason Selk. He is a psychologist turned coach who has helped many professional athletes and business people reach their goals. He believes that our brains are hardwired to succeed when we see something happen in advance. He has a 90 second daily mental exercise that has helped me see my future.

1. He says he starts by breathing in for 5 seconds, hold for 2 seconds, then breathe out for 7 seconds. This settles the heart rate and clears the mind.

2. Then Selk recommends that a person state 3 or 4 main things from vision as if he or she already has become those things. (For example, I might say: I put God first, I have a Boston Marathoning family, I overachieve on my client's expectations, and I am an awesome mission president)

3. In his mind, Dr. Selk then goes through his vision statement, visualizing it occurring. He notices how he feels as it is happening. In his mind, he plays the video of himself living it, using as many senses as he can, Noticing how he feels accomplishing it. (Currently I see myself jacked up running through the finish line at the Boston Marathon with my arms raised high, crowd cheering, with a big smile, celebrating the accomplishment)

4. Finally, he goes through his next day from beginning to end, reminding himself of the things that are part of the processes that will work toward accomplishing his vision.

5. Then he repeats step 2.

6. And he repeats step 1.

Jason Selk has stated that this process will train the subconscious mind to work on our conscious minds to accomplish what we desire. When we go through the same vision statement every night, through repetition, we begin to see it happening in our future. Our minds have turned our vision from a dream to reality.

The third step to seeing one's future is to pray. I talk with God right after I go through my visualization exercise. Talking with God helps me gain confidence in the future. I find that most of my important goals don't happen without first going through some difficult situation that makes me want to give up on it. There are times that I almost laugh at elements of my vision when I am going through the exercise, because my current circumstances are so far off that it seems crazy to see it in the future. In my talks with God I feel like I gain perspective and am able to move forward. God brings me back to see all things are possible and if I just focus on the process everything will work out.

Of course, we need to work towards our vision. We won't be able to visualize our dreams for long if we don't work towards it. Working toward it is not that complicated. Don't worry about performance so much. Just do it. I have always told my kids, "90% of life is showing up." When we show up for work we are more likely to improve in our work. When we show up at the gym we are more likely to get in better shape. When we show up for church we are more likely to worship. If we just show up on a regular basis to whatever we are working toward, it is amazing what will happen.

A day from my junior year illustrates this point. At this stage in my life my goals and vision of high school were to "be the friendliest guy in the room," stay out of trouble, and excel in sports. I had accomplished this by focusing on being around great friends and having very little drama in my high school years. I didn't really think I had any enemies.

One day, I was in my high school math class. We had a test, which wasn't always the most fun, but we just tried to get through it. As I started answering the questions a small high school kid that I did not know came to the door and asked for David Shuley. My teacher nodded to me that it was all right to go out and talk to him. As I walked out of the classroom the door shut behind me, the little kid who asked to speak to me was gone. Instead, there was a big muscular student rushing toward me. His face was enraged and he was bouncing around like Rocky Balboa looking for a fight. He had two large friends that got behind me to block the door so I could not return to class. He was yelling at me telling me I had told Elaine (his girlfriend) that he was a partier. Apparently they had broken up the previous night and my name was brought up. Six months earlier while at a cross-country camp, I had asked her "Why are you dating him, I hear he is a party guy and uses drugs." She was not that kind of girl.

He was as mad as a hornet now and wanted to fight. I told him I hardly know him and have no desire to fight. As I turned to go back into the classroom his friends pushed me back out. I was stuck.

His anger grew as he was bouncing around continuously taunting me to fight. I didn't know what to do. I was saying to myself, "How can I get out of this?" Then without seeing it coming he popped me square in the nose. Blood splattered to my shoulder from the blow. It happened so quickly I was stunned. Not being a fighter I had no instincts to retaliate. I just felt numb all over, especially in the nose region.

He was still bouncing around ready for more when a popular football player who walked upon the scene said for him to get out of here. They left me alone to my mushy nose.

I immediately walked down to the bathroom as my nose was leaking blood and other fluids. It was like an open faucet. My nose felt as soft as my cheek. I figured it was broken because it has never felt that way before.

It was so soft to the touch. I worked on it for 15 minutes in the bathroom trying to clean it out. After a while, I felt composed enough so I went back to my math class. As I walked in the class I was amazed that no one had heard any of the commotion going on right outside the door. I casually walked to my desk and began to take my exam. I did not do so well on that exam. It was a little hard to focus. I had to sniff many times to keep my nose from dripping onto my test paper. I finally completed it and the bell rang to end the class.

As the class ended I asked Brian if he knew what had happened. He had not said a word during the test. He assumed I went to the principal's office and received the news that a family member had died. He thought I was holding back all the tears with my sniffling. He was amazed when I told him the story.

It would have been a macho story had I responded to the first punch with a return uppercut that took him down. But instead I just stood there shocked really not having a fighting instinct in my body. Most would say, "What a wimp." I get why they could think that. But for me, this is where confidence in my vision and myself made all the difference. When I was in that moment, my vision of being the friendliest guy in the room kept me from fighting back. (Frankly, it wasn't that hard to be the friendliest guy in that room.) When we have a vision of friends, no drama, no enemies, there will inevitably be something that will test us.

In this case instead of saying "What's wrong with me?" I said to myself, "That guy has some problems. I hope things work out for him. It is not about me." I was not bitter.

The next day he came to my locker to say he was sorry. He was quite humble about it. I was good so I promptly forgave him. He probably did it to save his life. Although I didn't plan to retaliate, after hearing my story, half the high school was ready to take him out.

So that was that. It was over. It didn't define me. I thought of myself as a good guy. My confidence allowed me to quickly move on and keep the vision of being the friendliest guy in the room. The fight didn't deter my vision of my future and myself. We cannot let bad things that happen to us define us or stop us from seeing ourselves as we have visualized it.

I feel many are stuck in what they feel has been dealt to them. They just endure life. I view it as a tragedy that few people do much to create the life they desire. Even though we all struggle through many difficulties that test us, we can do much to design our lives to be filled with what we want in it.

Henry David Thoreau once said "If one advances confidently in the direction of his dreams, and endeavors to live the life which he has imagined, he will meet with a success unexpected in common hours. He will pass an invisible boundary; new, universal, and more liberal laws will begin to establish themselves around and within him; and he will live with the license of a higher order of beings."

This chapter's message is very important to me. If we internalize its message we will create a life that we have dreamed. If you can only see it, eventually it will happen!

Questions to consider: Have I created a written vision for my future? Do I have a process to focus on it daily?

CHAPTER 5

Joy Emerges from Service

"To enjoy the journey is to leap into people's lives. To enjoy the journey is to give until the stretch is a sacrifice. The question always is: what is it in life that will pull you out of your seat to be brave, risk and serve?" —Janie Jasin

I swerved through the crowded roller rink as the beat of the song "YMCA" blasted through the speakers. People were shoulder to shoulder wobbling around the oval trying to stay up on their skates. The smell of popcorn and treats filled the crowded air making it a perfect scene for teenage fun. I felt in control, making my way through the throngs of skaters. In the organized chaos, the speed of the crowd was a little too much for some. But for me, I loved to race my friends as if it were a track meet weaving through the peloton.

On one of my high-speed turns I saw my mother rolling along. She had been kind enough to take us skating and had even chosen to participate. She was a beginner that looked ready to fall 90% of the time. As I approached her on the turn I noticed a problem developing. As she skated along, she did not turn sharp enough and was headed directly for the wall. There was nothing I could do. This was going to hurt. Within a split second, she hit the wall square and went down to the floor. She had smacked her head hard against the wall, which put her in an instant daze.

As I rolled up she was circled about by all who were concerned. The blow made her sound drunk as she tried to explain what happened. She lay on her back for a couple minutes to collect herself. We lifted her up to her feet and slowly brought her to a place where she could sit down.

She was done.

People gave her some painkillers to stop the headache/concussion. As she rested, we continued to skate and enjoy our time. When it was over, we all piled into the lima bean colored Ford Bronco which was the family car at the time. This was a large car with very stiff suspension and big snow tires. It was loud, ugly, and an uncomfortable ride.

On the way home we stopped to get some fast food. We went through the drive-through to save some time. Judging from the way my mom spoke to the attendant and paid for the meal, her head was still not clear. I looked at my siblings with my eyes wide open. We all thought we had a drunk driver on our hands, and she didn't even know it. After we got our food, we started to pull out of the parking lot. The Bronco was elevated high enough that in her medicated state she didn't notice missing the exit. Instead, she drove straight through and over the bushes lining the curb. With her speed she never stopped, taking out all the shrubbery along the way. This happened just before the car launched off the tall curb. We came down hard and began bouncing out of control. We almost hit our heads on the ceiling, with the stiff suspension in the no seat belts era. My mom did her best to correct and settle the car, this while trying to avoid hitting the other vehicles on the busy street. In answer to a quick prayer we did not hit anything or anybody, and our car settled into the normal driving line toward our home.

When we arrived home, mom went straight to bed. Her headache persisted for a couple of days but that did not stop her from performing her normal motherly duties. With three teenage kids there was too much going on for her to slow down. She just gutted her way through it like most great mothers would do. With today's science around concussions it would have been viewed far more seriously. But especially as a youth, I didn't think anything of it. This was just my normal mother who always took care of us and put her children first in her life. Now as I look back on those days, I know she was not just a mom, she was a saint.

My mother is one of the greatest examples of service I have ever met.

My mother grew up in southeast Texas in a small town of Orange. She lived there until she moved to Houston during high school. She grew up in a southern well to do home with an African American maid that she adored. Her parents loved her and took care of her. But when it was time to make a decision about college she wanted to go as far away as she could.

She had taken a road trip in high school with a family friend to Utah and saw the BYU campus. She fell in love with it, even though it was a private religious school that was not of her faith. She thought that the people she met lived in a way that was more to her conservative liking. Her parents were not a fan of the distance but she was determined and they acquiesced.

It was at BYU where my mom and dad met, fell in love, and got married. Although my mom went to two years of school, she abandoned her goal of finishing her bachelor's degree so that she could support my dad as he started his career. They moved to California and then on to Washington to start their family.

My mother has always been my moral compass. I have memories of her making simple mistakes, but I have no memory of her ever doing something wrong. Jessica Lange once said, "The natural state of motherhood is unselfishness." My mother's entire adult life has been devoted to the service of others. I didn't notice many activities devoted to just her wellbeing. Everything she did seemed to be for the family and especially for the kids. I would suppose she was typical for most good mothers. She cooked meals, created our agenda for the day, was a taxi driver, was the religious rock in the home, was the person to whom we went when we got hurt; she basically took care of all our daily needs. We didn't think anything of it.

To illustrate this point, when I was a high school senior I struggled with track. I had started off the indoor season winning the races throughout the state. I was prepared to have a fabulous finish to my high school career. After about a month of winning races I felt a burning sensation in my Achilles on a February morning run.

I had never been injured before. It really frustrated me. I had to stop running for a few weeks to let it heal. It took me out of the biggest indoor meets of the season. But even worse, I wasn't able to run high mileage for my base training needed for the outdoor season. I didn't start running again until late March when the season was already under way. I was in no shape for distance.

When I started racing again, instead of winning races, I was in the middle of the pack. I found myself finishing with freshman and other underclassmen that for years had not been in my league. It was a humbling experience for me to say the least.

I did my best to improve as the season progressed. I found myself struggling in most of the longer races. At one of the biggest track meets of the year, the coach put me as the finishing 800-meter leg of the medley relay. It was with some underclassmen that were not fast. I had already underperformed in the two mile that day, so this was just to help out the young guys. I had no expectations.

I was almost in last place when I received the baton after the first two runners had run their 200 meters and the third runner had run 400 meters. I took off as hard as I could go. I was so far behind it would take a lot to catch up.

I had not run such a short distance that season. What I found is that it didn't take much endurance for the 800 compared to the 2 mile. My natural ability just kicked in. I started passing people one after the other. It almost felt like old times as I ran fast without any element of doubt. I really enjoyed passing the runners. As I rounded the final turn there was one more guy to catch. He was about 10 yards ahead. When I saw him begin to tighten up, I pushed it as hard as I could. As we neared the finish I was almost there. I gave it one last final push and leaned in to the finish. My lean got him by an inch. It was more like a dive as I fell to the ground. Totally exhausted I lay there until someone came to help me up. When they did so, I noticed my right shoulder wince with a quick sharp pain.

My teammates were thrilled to get their only medal of the year. I was pleased to finally have a good race. It gave me hope that in 3 weeks when state occurred maybe I could still compete.

I went home a few hours later when the track meet ended. I needed to take a shower and get ready for the evening. When I started to pull my racing jersey over my head, something crazy happened. My right arm fell out of its socket and hung out from my side. Literally I looked like an alien. Instead of my arm hanging from my shoulder area, it protruded from the side of my lower ribs. It had dislocated from the fall at the finish of the race. When I had raised my arm up to take off my shirt, gravity took its course.

It didn't hurt too badly at first. My first thought was I needed to show this to my mother. I went upstairs yelling for her. She was talking with a friend in the family room. As I walked in and gave her the freak show, she quickly said goodbye to her friend. Alarmed, she grabbed my dad and quickly got me into the car to go to the hospital.

The ride over was where the pain really came on. My arm began to throb. Every bump the car hit would jolt me with pain. I was in complete agony. To this day, I have never been in more physical pain.

When we arrived at the hospital there was a long wait. There had been a major car accident and I was not the top priority. My arm hurt so much and now I was just sitting there waiting. Finally the doctor came in and told me I would need to be knocked out to put the shoulder back in place. So they gave me the anesthesia and I was gone. Apparently when I was unconscious, my dad almost fainted, watching the procedure. The doctor grabbed my arm and at the same time he put his foot into my armpit. Then he turned and pulled my arm with a jerk. It was back into place.

When I woke up, I found myself groggy and looked down to discover my arm in a sling. I asked my parents how long I would need to have the sling on, because the state track meet was 3 weeks away and it would be hard to run with it. They looked at me and said, "Your track season is over. This will take over a month to heal." When I heard those words, all the emotions, frustrations, and heartaches that had built up my senior year came to a head. I just burst out crying with emotion. I bawled like a baby. It was over. My high school running career was over. All I could feel was extreme disappointment. As I cried, my mom sat in silence and gave me the longest hug trying her best to console me.

For most of high school, my mom would come to my room before bed and tickle my back while reading one chapter of the scriptures and talk about the day. It was a habit I loved because I got so relaxed before bed. Sometimes I heard very little of the scriptures because her presence comforted me and I drifted right off to sleep. This act of service, at such a formative age, I have never forgotten.

Well, that night I needed my mom. My arm hurt, I was depressed, and I had to figure out a way to move on. As she began tickling my back I started to relax. All I remember after that is her listening ear. I talked about all the things that had happened to me and she provided me the needed perspective. I needed her to be there. The bedtime routine provided the perfect environment for my healing.

The next few days were not good. But within a couple weeks, even though I still had a bitter taste in my mouth I was able to move on and get excited about graduation.

My mother is one of the greatest examples of service in my life. She always took care of us, and those around her. She was always there when I needed her. She loved her family so much. It showed in how much she served us. Mitch Album said, "Love is when you are as concerned about someone else's situation as your own." Doesn't that personify most great mothers out there? It certainly reflected mine.

I think we can learn a tremendous amount from our mothers. One of the greatest lessons is the cause and effect of service. Isn't it interesting, that there is no one that moms serve more than their children? Also, there is no one that our mother had more love for than her children. Service creates deep love in a person's life. It is a true principle that personifies itself most clearly in the parent/child relationship.

I have met many people who feel they have no love in their lives. They feel no one loves them. They may have few quality relationships. It isn't always an easy fix, but what I know is that it starts with serving someone or some cause. Without service I have found it difficult to have deep love in life. Additionally, I believe that joy actually emerges from service. When we serve, we experience love and joy.

My opportunity to serve in a meaningful way came after my graduation from high school. Even though I was generally very happy in high school and felt it was one of my favorite periods of my life, there was only a small amount of service. I had good friends, school activities, religious leaders, self-esteem, and an occasional girlfriend to spend time with, but most things were focused around me, not others.

For years I had expected to serve a mission for The Church of Jesus Christ of Latter Day Saints. I had looked forward to it. It had been a goal of mine from the age of 12. After the summer of my graduation year, the time had come. I filled out the required paperwork and received a call from the church to serve in the San Antonio, Texas mission. I would serve for two years with other missionaries, sharing the Gospel of Christ to all who would listen.

Like most things in life, things didn't start out exactly as expected. Two nights before I was supposed to enter into the missionary training center, I decided to play basketball with some friends. It would be the last time hanging out with them for quite a while. They were all ballers, which would make it a perfect final night together.

We never held back on the basketball court. We had played together for years. As friends we talked smack and went at each other hard. I played guard up top in a zone defense. I was quick, which allowed me to steal the ball quite often. During one play that night I saw an opportunity for a steal. During the opponent's pass I reached forward and tapped the ball forward to run and grab it for a fast break layup.

For some reason, my shoulder was in an awkward position when I tapped the ball, and I felt my shoulder come out of its socket. I had not had any problems with my shoulder for the past seven months since it originally had come out. I had played basketball numerous times, body surfed in the ocean waves, wrestled with my friends, and many other active things, while not once having any problems. But this night, my arm hung in that awkward position. The last night with my friends was to be spent in the ER.

This time, it wasn't as painful snapping my arm back into place. The doctor did it without medication. He just said, "This will hurt but only for a split second." He grabbed my arm then simultaneously twisted and pulled. It hurt, but quickly the pain was gone and my arm was back in the socket. He told me I needed to go to a doctor the next day to have it checked out.

The following day, the orthopedic surgeon suggested that going forward, my shoulder was so loose that without surgery it would continuously fall out of place. So we decided to have surgery the next day to place a pin in my shoulder to keep it in place. The day I was supposed to start my mission I was now headed for the OR.

The surgery went well. I had to rest for 4 days before the pain from the surgery would be low enough to consider entering the missionary training center. It was aggressive but I started my mission with a sling and a smile still taking pain pills every few hours.

The missionary training center in Provo, Utah had over two thousand missionaries being trained to serve in places throughout the world. Those going to foreign lands began to learn the languages. For my mission in Texas, I was going to spend 2 ½ weeks learning how to teach people in a way that they could understand.

My first day was rough. I felt weak and nauseated. Trying to pay attention in the classroom was daunting. I just felt like lying down. But after a few days, things started to turn around. Even though I couldn't workout or shower like everyone else, I was able to pay attention in class without feeling gross. By the end of the 2½ weeks I was out of the sling and charged up ready to start my new adventure in Texas.

When I arrived in Texas I was an energetic, naive, young missionary. I had a testimony that I felt could make a difference in someone's life. I was bursting at the seams to share it. When I met my companion we got to work the very first day. I found the lifestyle to be something I could adapt to quickly.

I soon found trying to share a message of Christ to others was harder than I thought. Some just felt I was crazy and others had no time for this sort of thing. About 50% of my time, I was putting myself out there and getting rejected. It wasn't too fun. About 35% of the time, it was really good where people treated me with kindness, fed us, and listened to us. About 15% of the time it was pure joy. The joy came when we taught them about Christ, and their life changed for the better. We showed them the way to feel God's love. These people were downtrodden, their life was a mess, they were without hope or faith, but we helped change that. That's what makes all the hard work and rejection of a mission worthwhile.

After a few months in San Antonio we met Tom and Tina. They were a couple in their late 50's. They had two grown children and a somewhat happy marriage. When we met them they had not really gone to a church as a family. They hadn't thought much about their faith until we met them. As we taught them about Christ, they felt the spirit in their home for the first time and they loved it. They wanted more and more every time we visited. I loved seeing the look in Tina's eyes every time we showed up. She treated us like we were angels.

Every visit ended with the same routine. They had two large German Shepherd dogs that shed hair throughout their house. Before leaving, we would stretch out our arms and legs like a shake down from a cop and she would tape roll us to get the hair off. Then we were on our way.

They accepted all aspects of the gospel without hesitation. As part of our faith we have a law of health where we do not smoke tobacco. For many, it is often a barrier to being baptized because it is so hard to quit. They both smoked two packs a day but they immediately decided to put the cigarettes away for good. This was not easy for them.

One day while we were teaching them, Tina was in a cranky mood. The lack of nicotine was really hitting her hard. She snapped at her dogs to get away from us because of the hair. I had never seen her raise her voice. I remember that day feeling bad for her. I wanted to help in some way. I was about to tell her to maybe have just one cigarette to calm her down. As I opened my mouth to say it, the spirit wrenched my heart and said "No, don't say that." It was almost a physical wrenching of the spirit. I had never been so directed from an outside source in what to say. I knew that God was directing me because it wasn't just an impression. God had told me on what was best for her. I didn't say a word.

They eventually stopped smoking. It rejuvenated their health. They didn't realize the effect smoking had had on many aspects of their lives. More importantly, during this time they gained a testimony of Christ that was real. The many new friends at church strengthened them, and because of this, they decided to be baptized.

As I stood in a baptismal font the day of Tom and Tina's baptism I felt pure joy. There was such a peaceful feeling in the air. We were dressed in white as I placed her in the water. When she came up out of the water, she smiled from cheek to cheek with happiness and love. The responding love I felt for Tina and Tom could only come through serving and bringing people to God.

As I mentioned earlier, serving creates love in our lives. We love those we serve. Tina is an important example of this in my life. I have also noticed that love seems to be even deeper for those we serve in a spiritual manner. Spiritual connection is a next level type of love. God+service=lasting love.

After the gospel changed Tom and Tina, they wanted their family to hear the message. I will never forget the moment I met their 26-year-old daughter. She was a beautiful girl with red hair that made a young man like me have a difficult time focusing on just teaching the gospel. Yet with her beauty, there was pain in her eyes. She looked worn out from the world. As she told us her story my mouth dropped in awe.

She was a stripper by profession; she lived with a guy, she smoked and drank heavily, and she felt nothing but pain in her life. She was lost.

We began by discussing how God loved her. How he had a plan for her. We taught her many truths that she could choose to live by, which would change her life. Her parents were part of the discussions. When her parents testified to her the changes they had made in their lives, she began to believe it was possible for herself.

It was amazing to witness the metamorphosis that happened right before our eyes. Over time she went from a girl who felt like she needed to use her body in life to be accepted, to someone who knew that she had God's DNA within her. She walked away from her old life and began her new life in Christ. What happiness it brought her, what joy it brought me! There is a great verse in the Book of Mormon in Mosiah 2:17 that says, "When you are in the service of your fellow beings, ye are only in the service of your God." Teaching her was serving her. Serving her was serving God. That is why lasting love and joy is produced so readily.

The coast of Corpus Christi, Texas 1988

One of the great things about serving a full time mission for two years without interruption is that there isn't any distraction. I didn't date. I didn't have a job and I wasn't attending school. All I did with my day was work hard to serve people. When our lives are devoted to service, another principle develops. I can explain it in a story that happened toward the end of my two years.

One hot summer evening, I was walking with my companion on the neighborhood streets of San Antonio. We had no appointments and thought it would be nice to find someone interested in hearing our message. We came upon a young Hispanic man in his early 20's. His name was Benjamin. He was just hanging out on his front lawn. We walked up to him and asked if he were open to hearing a message about Christ. He agreed.

We sat on white plastic chairs in his front yard, as the setting sun began to allow relief from the heat. We got to know Benjamin a little bit, and we found out that he was a saxophone player. He was a single college student who loved nothing more than playing his music.

After getting to know him, we shared a Gospel message that we had told a hundred times. There was nothing remarkable about the visit. We were probably there around 45 minutes. He seemed to enjoy it and the Spirit was present.

After setting a return appointment to see him again, we said goodbye. As we turned to walk away he stopped us. He had something he wanted to share with us. We walked back to him. In a reverent tone he said, "I want you guys to know that before you came tonight I had a dream about you. I knew you would come." I was astonished. I asked him, "When did you have this dream?" He said, "About a month ago." I asked, "Did we look like this?" He said, "Yes, you had white shirts and ties on just like you do now." I marveled at the thought. We were in one of his dreams. How incredible.

We then thanked him for sharing this with us and walked away. As we went home, my companion and I were stoked. We talked about how cool this experience was for us. We felt he would be in a great place to hear our message in the coming days because God had prepared him.

That night, before I went to bed, I couldn't get the thought of this out of my head. I thought of what I was doing a month ago. At that time, unbeknownst to me, God placed us in someone's dream to prepare him for our message. God used us both as a tool or instrument for His work without us even knowing about it.

Benjamin went on to be baptized a few weeks later. He did this on his own without support from his friends or family. He just knew this was something God wanted for him in his life. I always thought this young saxophone player was one the coolest converts of my mission. Maybe it was the one earring he had in his ear, which wasn't the norm in the late 80's. Maybe it was his saxophone. He just had a vibe about him when he walked into the room. I was blessed to be a part of his story.

Benjamin's baptism was such a memorable day.

What Benjamin's story illustrates is that when we have a focus of service in our lives, God will use us as a tool—a tool in something that is bigger than just ourselves. He will put us in the paths of others to make an impact. We will be instruments for good. Serving as an instrument for God is the best kind of service.

As a result of being used by God, our lives will have joy and lasting love. This joy and love is what everyone is looking for but many folks have a difficult time finding. I want to shout from the rooftops and say, "If you don't have enough love in your life, start with service."

A question to consider: Is service a big part of my daily life?

CHAPTER 6

All Because Two People Fell In Love

"I live for those who love me, for those who know me true." —George Linnaeus Banks

My date stepped down into the jacuzzi with her tight swimsuit clinging to her body. The steam was rising out of the bubbles creating a mystical scene. As I looked up at her, my mind was going crazy and my body was buzzing. I hadn't been on a date in over two years, much less sitting in a jacuzzi with a beautiful girl. Missionaries do not swim for safety reasons so except to baptize I hadn't been in water for a long time. Now I am in a jacuzzi with a girl on my first post mission date.

I was way over my head. I sat in the water trying not to get caught staring or looking nervous. I tried to have a normal conversation. But what is normal? For two years the majority of my conversations were about the gospel. What would I talk about? This was not exactly the best environment to bring up Jesus. I am sure my date laughed a little inside as she saw me squirm. I tried my best with the conversation but it most likely sounded a lot like a guy trying to get a girl to like him.

It is interesting to not date for 2 complete years. It creates some withdrawals. What I have found with most of my missionary friends is that we are like a dog in heat right after a mission. Luckily we had taught morals for two years so our intentions were good ones. We were just in constant pursuit for that next date with one purpose in mind: to get married. For the first time in our lives we have been given the green light.

I went to BYU for college. One thing unique about this school is that a third of the 33,000-student body are married. Utah has the youngest marital age of the entire country. It is part of the culture to be looking to marry while in college. I had a goal to get married within the first 6 months upon my return from Texas. I was only a second semester freshman and 21 years old. Wow, what a thought.

Instead of 6 months it would take me 6 years to marry. The delay wasn't from the lack of effort. I went out most weekends and sometimes multiple times in a week. I made many dating and relationship mistakes along the way. I also had fun and learned many things about what I wanted in a wife. Even though by the end of my single life I was very tired of it all, I would not have wanted it to turn out any differently than it did.

Having said that, I wish someone would have explained to me a few things about dating and finding a wife that would have made it more fulfilling along the way. Choosing a spouse is the most important decision we ever make in our life. It can be a source of great joy or heartache depending on how that choice turns out.

There are no guarantees that the one we choose will be the spouse of our dreams. But we can improve the odds by not beginning our marriage with many difficulties that exist with certain couples. It is important to look for someone to whom we are attracted, one we can be ourselves around and, best of all, one who will influence us to be better. These principles are very important.

Over the 6 years of post mission dating, I had no problem finding girls to be attracted to. That was the easy part. Because I had no problem asking a girl for a date, I went out most weeks. Prior to marriage, I may have gone out with around 200 different girls. The hard part was to find someone I could be myself around. For most of my dating I tried to impress girls so that they would "really" know me and understand what a great guy I was. I had a hard time just being myself and letting conversations unfold naturally. As a result, in all of those dates, I only had relationships with three girls in college and about four after college. The longest lasting around six months.

I spent a lot of time with these college buddies. We played football during the day and went on dates together at night.

In my first year of college after my mission I had a crush on a girl. I wanted to impress her. Instead of taking her to dinner and a movie I felt I had to make a splash. So I contacted a friend of mine whose uncle was a private pilot. I convinced him to go on a double date where we would fly up Provo Canyon for a 25-minute flight and land in the small town of Heber City. We would go over to a resort to swim and then to my friend's aunt's house for dinner. I went to the farthest lengths to impress.

When I picked up my date, she seemed excited to go. I thought of how impressed she must be with me for creating such a day. When we entered the small 4-seat plane there was nervousness in both of us. We had not been in a private plane before. As we took off and headed up the canyon, the white snow capped mountains were beautiful. As we looked out the window I pointed out certain pretty views to my date. It was fun seeing such a great scene up close. I thought to myself, "This date is going well." She must be impressed.

After we landed and got into the car to go to the resort to swim, I began to notice a change in her vibe. The look of awe and excitement in her eyes was dissipating. The flight was over and now it was just a drive in a car. The conversation began to drag. Of course, I micro analyzed everything throughout the date and my radar went up. What typically happened next was I started to fill the holes in the conversation. I tried to impress her by trying to tell her all about myself. Impress, impress, impress. That is what I was all about.

Well, the swim didn't go much better and by dinner I was saying to myself, "Why doesn't she like me that much? I had tried so hard. I had planned such fun activities. What went wrong?"

This was a common situation I found myself in during my dating years. I think I would have done better in relationships if I had followed some of the advice found in the movie "Hitch." Will Smith played a role as a relationship guru where he helped unlikely guys end up with the women of their dreams. He said, "When you're wondering what to say or how you look, just remember, she's already out with you. That means she said yes when she could have said no. That means she made a plan when she could have just blown you off. So that means it's no longer your job to make her like you. It's your job not to mess it up."

I have found in the singles scene, our dates do not need elaborate entertaining events. They just need an environment for us to get to know each other. People want to have relationships with those who aren't needy. Often we are most attracted to the person who is initially not too overly impressed—someone who is respectful on the date and feels a comfortable equal. Mature people want to date those that are perfectly happy without them but want and choose to be with them. Those that could walk away from the relationship and still be happy. That is what is attractive to people. It is the opposite of what I tried to do each date.

Docked on the shore of Lake Powel on one of my 18 college road trips.
Dating seemed easy, relationships not so much.

When I finally met my wife Tonya, I was just coming off a 3-month relationship with a girl who went away to college. I still liked the girl, but she didn't want to be tied down with a long distance relationship. Tonya had broken off an engagement the year before to a guy she still loved but knew it was not a right fit for marriage. So even though I thought she was cute, when we sat at dinner, neither one of us were too worried about it working out.

I remember Tonya looking at me straight in the eye with complete confidence saying, "Why aren't you married yet?" She was basically saying, "What is the matter with you?" She felt it odd since I had established myself in my career and was reasonably good looking that I was still available. "There must be something wrong with him." I had no answer for her but at that moment I felt she was an equal and not just another girl.

We started hanging out together almost every day. She was easy to talk to and fun to be with. Normally at this phase I would be head over heels for the girl, impressing her daily with my kindness and charm. But even though we both liked each other we were both not acting weird because we had old relationships that were still in our hearts. It made it friendlier in the beginning and neither one of us were there only to impress. We could be ourselves.

After seeing each other daily for a while, the feelings really began to grow. We then wrote off our past relationships. The word love started coming up in conversation. We wanted the same things. We both wanted kids, we were both open for her to be in the home to help raise them. We had the same faith. We both had served in missions. We enjoyed nature and hiking the great outdoors. I found she had a great capacity to feel the emotions for other people and therefore succor them. This is not a quality I had too much of, so I knew I would be a better person around her.

I began this book with a theme that, "We become who we hang out with." Those we fall in love with have a 10x influence compared to regular friends. They really can influence us positively or negatively in big ways. I have seen many situations where reason quickly goes out the window because of the influence of those we love. I feel this is especially true in the physical elements of dating. People sometimes will do things they would have never considered because of the influence of those they are in a relationship with. It is so important in this decision that we pick people who have similar morals, who respect us, and who are living lives we can admire and aspire to.

Tonya and I were on the same page with all of these things. So it was a natural consequence to want to marry her. I had tried to get married for 6 years. Most of my friends were married. I had a career. I had my own apartment. I was independent from my parents. I was tired of the dating scene and wanted to settle down. From all my years of dating I knew what I wanted in a spouse. It was simply the right time for me. I know all marriages don't have perfect timing for everyone. I don't think there are checklists that need to happen before one can consider marriage. But in my case, having so many things in place from a timing perspective eliminated many challenges that some people experience.

The day came for the big ask. While Tonya was at work, I went over to her home to ask her father for permission to take her hand in marriage. We went on a drive to have a quick chat. He had no problem and really didn't ask much. The only thing I remember him saying is, "What do you think Tonya will say?" I hadn't considered that she would say "No." In fact, I had already reserved the Salt Lake Temple for the wedding date. But from that point on the rest of the day I was a nervous wreck wondering what she would say.

After getting the OK from my future father-in law I went to Walmart to buy a cubic zirconium. I bought it because I felt that I wanted her to put a ring on her finger when I proposed but still wanted her to pick out her diamond for the real ring. That was my way of accomplishing both goals. After my $86 purchase, I pulled out of the parking stall and backed into another car. This placed a large dent in the back quarter panel of my car. This only added to the stress of my day.

When the night came I was so excited. I took her to the best restaurant in town with a beautiful view of the city. I found myself nervous at dinner. Tonya even asked about what was wrong and I just shrugged it off. She had no idea that I was going to ask her for her hand that night.

After dinner we drove to the Devou Park lookout. It was a clear cold 10-degree night where the city lights just sparkled. When we got out of the car, I grabbed the thick blanket that had roses wrapped inside and began walking toward the benches. She immediately asked for the blanket because of the cold. I told her I would give her it at the benches, which slightly irritated her.

When we arrived at the bench I didn't waste any time. I got down on one knee and said, "Tonya, will you marry me?" She paused for a second, which seemed like an eternity, and then said, "Yes." What a relief. My worries of the day were for naught. She wanted to marry me! We sat and had the greatest conversation about our plans to marry. After 6 years of searching there was no better conversation!

The day before our wedding was such an exciting day!

Seven weeks later, the night before the wedding, I dropped Tonya off at her downtown Salt Lake City hotel room to say goodnight. I wouldn't see her again until the ceremony. I went into her room and sat on the edge of the bed. We talked for a minute and then began to make out. After kissing a few minutes I started to get heated up. Even though we had made out many times, this time I felt rather tempted to go further. Heck she was going to be my wife. But instead, I decided I needed to get out of there. I said goodnight and told her how excited I was about tomorrow. As I walked out the door into the hotel hallway I raised both hands above my head in victory like Rocky Balboa at the top of the steps in Philadelphia. I had done it. I had saved myself for my wedding night. Tonya had as well. Now, tomorrow was my wedding day. No more holding back!

Through all the years of dating I had kissed a few girls and was tempted many times to go further. But I had always had a goal to save myself until I was married. It was hard at certain times but I did it. That night I knew that the wait was officially over. What a great feeling. It is one of the biggest accomplishments of my life.

Looking back, I feel that saving myself has allowed me early on to have a deeper relationship, deeper conversation, deeper understanding of what's important to my spouse without it mostly being about the physical. I am so thankful I made this a goal.

I think there is more than one way to save yourself for your wife. An experience from a couple years prior will illustrate. I had been asked to go to a bachelor party for a family member. I had been to various bachelor parties with friends from college. They had not been the typical parties you would think about. It consisted mostly of poker, jokes, and good fun with friends.

I was not ignorant about this particular party. I knew there would be a lot of drunks by the end of the night. But all the dads would be there so I didn't think too much about it. I went to the party and played some baseball. I don't drink but am not bothered the majority of the time with those drinking around me.

The night was a lot of fun hanging out and playing some games. As the night went on it got a bit rowdy from the alcohol consumption but I wasn't bothered by it. I guess I would make a good designated driver.

At one point they decided to have everyone gather inside to hand out some presents. Obviously some of those gifts you wouldn't want to show your mother. But they were all just for fun. The groom was having a great time.

Then at a certain point, they said "get ready" the stripper has arrived. I guess most bachelor parties in America include this but because this was a family party I never thought this was going to be included.

I sat there in the room with all of these juiced up men, thinking, "Do I really want to see this?" My body was telling me, "Stay, stay, stay." My spirit was telling me, "Get the heck out of here." I sat there in this moment of truth. No one would think anything of it if I stayed. It would be less awkward to stay then to get up and leave. Did I really want this experience etched in my head? I know the images would never leave me.

I finally decided to bolt out the door. I didn't make a scene; I just walked out, headed to my car, and drove off. As I drove home all I could feel was anger. I was so mad that I was at an extended family party but yet everyone else's morals were so different that I had to be by myself. I had to feel isolated. I was on my own for the rest of my Saturday night.

The next day I talked to my family and asked them what had happened. They said when the stripper came; she eventually got completely nude dancing for all of these guys. I am sure most of them loved it. I am sure it created a great fantasy for them. For me, I thought something that day that I found later to be very significant. I thought to myself, "I guess I saved those images for my future wife."

Pornography is a great business. It obviously is not just for bachelor parties. It is found in movies and the internet today in a way that it is difficult to escape. It is estimated that the revenues from porn are larger than the NBA and Netflix combined.

I have certainly not been a perfect example in my life of staying away from porn. But what I have done is make it a focus to keep my mind as clean as possible. Today, I must keep working daily at staying away from all the things that take me down that path.

Maintaining purity of thought is a very crucial discipline for all of us. Studies are beginning to indicate that pornography is second only to unemployment in being a devastating self-esteem buster for men. Sadly, those who are addicted to porn often experience a dramatic decrease in their confidence with relationships and in their own self-confidence and self-respect. Researchers are beginning to find that pornography does something that is harmful to the psyche, and the images can stick with us forever.

I feel this is a sacrifice we can make for our future spouses, as well as for our future children. This can have a great impact on the integrity of our relationships and on the quality of our thought life, in general. It also will make saving yourself for marriage that much easier.

There are many resources that can be utilized if one feels addicted at this time. A good start is recognizing we all can do better. Almost every man I know has had a problem with this at one time or another in his life. It is part of the natural man. Our physical bodies crave sex in all of its forms. But all of us can overcome this.

Part of this life's test is for the spirit within us to control our physical bodies versus our physical bodies controlling our spirit. That is true freedom. Porn and sex are a big part of this challenge and they will be for the rest of our lives.

I have a good friend who once said to me, "I envy an element about your marriage. I see Tonya and you being able to talk about anything; whether it is family, morals, faith, or other sensitive subjects, you seem to be able to have that dialogue." He stated that his marriage is great, but because they were like "two rabbits physically" at the beginning of their relationship, they never developed the ability to talk at a deep level in some areas that are important to him.

This comment impressed me because most people would look at his marriage with praise because they deeply love each other. They have really worked at their marriage. But my thought is, "Why not start with the best possible beginning?"

Our wedding day! This was one of the best days of my life.

On our wedding day, as I gazed into Tonya's eyes, tears welled up in mine. We knelt across from the temple altar holding hands in the sealing room of the beautiful Salt Lake City Temple. In the Church of Jesus Christ of Latter Day Saints the marriage ceremony is a little unique. We exchange vows not standing but kneeling across an altar. We believe when married we are sealed together for eternity. The temple has mirrors on opposite walls which when you stand together it reflects your image going into eternity together. The imagery overwhelmed me in the moment. As I looked at her it felt so real, so good. As we exchanged marriage vows the feeling was both romantic and spiritual at the same time. It was a very unique sensation. They say that love between two people can create great things. But when you add God to the mix, the possibilities are limitless. He makes everything more grand. This event was a grand scene in my life. I couldn't ask for a better way, a better time, and a better place to commit my love to her forever.

Keeping a Happy Marriage

I had a desire to get married for about 6 years before I met Tonya. The amount of time it took to meet her was a trial. But after the wedding, I found married life easy. Our first 2 years felt like one long date. Not saying goodbye at the door at the end of the evening was a great perk. I have heard that some people, at first, have a hard time getting used to each other. That was not the case for us. We didn't have many arguments and we had fun without needing anyone else around to help. My parents were probably a bit offended by the lack of visits. We just enjoyed being alone together.

I wrote in my journal after nine months of marriage, "What a wonderful time of life this is! My relationship with Tonya has never been better. We are such good friends; we laugh, goof around, and make love, all that good stuff. It amazes me more and more each day how much we are alike. We both enjoy walking, seeing beautiful things, talking, experiencing spiritual growth, etc... I find that exciting because we are always together. I feel many couples are jealous of us. Our goal is to make everybody gag the rest of our lives from being too mushy. This weekend I am leaving for 4 days to go to the Homestead resort. This will be the first night away from her this year. That will be different. I look forward to the trip; I just wish she could come. She is just so gorgeous. I always thought I would end up with someone cool, but didn't know if I would get sexy too."

This is what love looks like, especially new love. There is something that occurs in the first two years of a relationship that is special. I guess the hormones are firing on all cylinders, which directed my thoughts constantly toward Tonya. I wanted to be with her 24/7. I could go shopping at the mall for hours and watch Tonya try on clothes and have a great time. But new love and mature love look somewhat different.

The combination of a shorter engagement and our first child not being born until 2 ½ years into the marriage enhanced those first two years of our relationship, making them among the most fun and happy times of my life. It was a time of life where we learned about what is important to each other, worked towards getting out of debt, bought our first home, traveled inexpensively to many places, learned how to communicate with each other, made plans for our life together, and never tired of affection.

What most people don't realize is that the infatuation you feel, the drive to be with your spouse 24/7, the frequent drive for sexual intimacy, and the love you feel comes naturally and easy for about two years. There comes a point after that where it requires focus, work, and effort for marriage to thrive.

This happens with or without kids in the mix. Children will exponentially increase the need for effort and focus. Kids' needs divert attention from each other and it is hard to serve two masters.

I think any person who is unhappy in marriage and is tempted by an affair would greatly benefit if they understood the principle of two years. They may feel their spouse isn't romantic like this new interest. They may not feel the same drive to be with their spouse like they do with their new interest. It looks greener on the other side, often because testosterone hides the many flaws of others. It seems their new love will produce the ride they are missing, until two years later when they find themselves right back where they were. Watching her try on clothes becomes torture again. With no driving force to keep them together, the sex gets ordinary and they are left with a person possibly not near as compatible as the first.

My spouse's well being is one of the most important responsibilities of my life. I feel that one of the first questions God will ask me on the other side is "How did you care for Tonya?" There is very little that matters more than this. It is one of the best gifts you can ever give your kids. They will model their marriage after yours most likely, good or bad.

This is why from the very beginning of marriage, it is important to focus on one's spouse. It's of great value to get into the habit of doing this when it's easy, to create routines that are meaningful and intimate when hormones will help drive you to do it anyway. It's important to set valuable patterns that can endure and enliven your marriage, even through the raising of children.

I will suggest three tips that I have focused on that are impactful to a successful, long lasting marriage. I am not suggesting this is an all-inclusive list. Nor may it be most important for you personally. These have just been some of my high priorities.

Choose To Date

I stood on the edge of the cliff, nervous and shaking. The thought of turning my back to the open void and leaning back had my mind racing. This was not just any cliff. It was a 130-foot drop off that went straight down for about 20 feet then cut inward for the rest of the drop. It would be 110 feet of free fall with nothing but ropes to save us.

I had come to Hocking Hills State Park for an adventurous date with Tonya. We had brought my friend Steve to take us repelling down the area's beautiful rock outcroppings. He was an expert mountain climber in whom we could have confidence that we wouldn't die having this fun.

He secured the ropes to a tree, dressed us with repelling gear, gave us some limited training, and then hopped off the edge confidently prancing down the wall. Once he hit the free fall area, all we could hear was the rope buzzing to the bottom.

Next Tonya, without showing an ounce of fear, hooked herself up and leaned back over the edge until she disappeared. I soon heard the sound of the rope as she flew to the bottom. She shouted at the bottom, "Steve that was awesome!" She made it look so easy. She demonstrated such bravery having never done this before. I was impressed. I also envied her because she had already completed the repel.

Now it was my turn. I was all alone up there with just my nerves and shaky legs. As I approached the edge, my body tightened with fear. There was a two-foot drop off a foot from the main ledge. I was so stiff and scared that I slipped and scraped my shins into a bloody mess. It stung but at that moment, all I could think about was the task at hand: lean back over the edge.

I shook and shook, standing there at the precipice. I said to myself, "Tonya just did it, I can do this. I have to do this." After a minute, I finally got the courage to hang out over the edge. I looked down and noticed how small they looked down there. That didn't help. Once secure, I started to walk down the wall. Then I pushed off more, going down about 10 feet. That part wasn't bad. But what about the free fall coming up? What if I got out of control and fell to my death?

When I arrived at the free fall, I began to go down, creating as tight of a hold as I could. I slowed down to almost a stop. Then I let loose some more. My insecurities began to fade away as I felt in control and glided at a reasonable pace to the bottom. When I touched my feet to the ground I felt a great sense of accomplishment. I did it. It was over. I didn't die. I gave them both a high five and didn't mention anything about my bloody shins.

Just getting warmed up on an easy 30 foot repel.

The long free fall scared me to death.

My weekly dates with Tonya have been one of the greatest elements of fun over the past 24 years. It is something to look forward to each week.

We don't always have creative dates. Sometimes it is just going out to eat. Sometimes it is just a long walk. Regardless of what we do, it is often the highlight of the week. Not much different to my single days when a good date was the best part of my week.

My experience suggests that if you are married, it's wise to go on a weekly date and see how much more fun your marriage can be. Even though I have always looked forward to it, I believe Tonya has looked forward to it even more. At times she has starved for moments to decompress with me. Married couples should not let dating stop once kids come. It can feel like a pressing excuse to stop taking time for a couple's night out, due to the needs of the children. But truthfully, a happy, fun, intimate marriage is one of the greatest gifts we can give our kids.

Friedrich Nietzsche once said, "It is not a lack of love, but a lack of friendship that makes unhappy marriages." I know of no better way to increase our friendship than to spend a generous amount of one on one time together. I find that the older our family gets, the busier we are, and sometimes our date is the only real deep conversation of the week. It is so important.

I want to bring up a dynamic for some couples that make dating in marriage very difficult. It is a psychological element that can occur when both spouses work full time and feel guilty being away from their kids. I can use the example of a conversation I had just the other day with a young friend of mine.

We were walking back to the office after lunch. This friend of mine has been married for four years with two kids under the age of three. He was discussing how crazy and tiring their life has been with a young family.

He has competed in multiple triathlons in the past. His wife is also athletic, but he said he doesn't have time to train anymore and is totally out of shape. He mentioned his wife signed up for a marathon a few months ago but gave up soon after because she felt so guilty taking the time away from her kids since she already worked full time. I asked about dating and he looked at me and said, "Are you kidding me?"

He went on to explain that he and his wife were worn out and tired with no way to recharge their batteries without feeling guilty. They were both already away from their children more hours in the week than they wanted to be. However, they had built their budgets around both of their incomes, so neither one could stop working.

As I listened to him, I realized one of the dynamics that allows Tonya and me to have a weekly date without worrying that we are giving up quality parent-child time is the fact that our children always have a parent around during the rest of the week. Our date night allows them freedom from us, which can be a refreshing change of pace for everyone.

I know that women are just as capable as any man, making decisions in the boardroom or running a Fortune 500 Company. They deserve opportunities and compensation equal to that of their male counterparts. In fact, some of my very best clients are female executives running large corporations. So, when I speak of a family choosing to have one parent in the home while raising children, I am not referring to capabilities or equal rights, nor am I being gender specific. I am merely referring to a lifestyle choice a family might make.

I have heard some say it minimizes the stature of a woman (or a man) to be called a stay at home parent. Tonya is often asked, "What do you do" and she admits it can feel uncomfortable not to have a corporate title or business role outside the home to refer to. However, I view her as the CEO of our home. She knows that raising children is a noble task, and she views the opportunity with pride and thankfulness.

Having said that, I know many two career families who do a wonderful job of balancing work life with loving parenting. There are also numerous single parents who work outside the home and manage parenting in a remarkable way. However, maintaining work/family balance is just harder without the consistence of one parent being available at home.

I know that having one spouse choose to stay at home with the kids is not the only factor in marital dating. There are many elements to work through. But whatever our circumstances, I cannot think of a more important choice to make than to choose to date our spouses forever.

Handle Disagreements Well

When thinking of a specific story to share regarding disagreements, my mind went to specific arguments of the past. Like being upset on a hike in Hawaii, or an argument in our bedroom, or a certain moment in the line at Disney World. But what's funny is: as I look back I cannot remember what the arguments were about. I really can't.

It's interesting that disagreements are seldom about something of great importance. Most of the time they are about nothing. Often, they occur because we are tired, or a little irritable from some situation at work, or stressed from money issues, or because we don't feel good about ourselves that day. Whatever it is, most arguments are not based on a large difference in opinions; rather, they are a result of some outside influence that is bugging us and we are irritable.

Regardless of why they happen, arguments are going to happen. I grew up never seeing my parents argue. Their disagreements always took place in private. They would go to their room to discuss things. I feel most comfortable having disagreements in private, probably because of what was modeled. Tonya, however, had parents who argued in front of her and she tends to feel that it is best not to hide disagreements.

I don't know if one way is better than the other. There are pros and cons to both. My parents allowed the feeling of peace in the home most of the time. But then one day they walked in, telling us they were separating. It created a lot of confusion. We didn't learn how to overcome difficulties because we never saw them. But yet the household prior to the separation was peaceful.

Tonya feels that when our kids see us disagree and make up, it gives them understanding of forgiveness and overcoming problems. They see the bad and then the good afterwards. Subsequently, in our marriage the majority of our disagreements have been out in the open.

I think whichever way a family chooses to deal with disagreements; there should be some rules of engagement. We have followed these quite well and have a better marriage because of it.

The first rule of engagement for arguments is: never call each other names. "You are an idiot." "You are a jerk." "You lazy bum." This is not helpful at all. It is important to talk about the issues and not get into labeling each other with negative titles. It doesn't do any good and actually creates a lot of harm. We should remember, words matter and name calling sticks.

The second rule is that we always say we are sorry afterwards. Tonya and I are both good at it. Without a heartfelt apology after an argument, it is very difficult for the relationship to get headed back in the right direction. What's most difficult is when I have felt that I am completely in the right but just know that the quickest way to a happy home is to be the one to say sorry first. It is hard but I have never regretted doing it. It isn't needed most of the time but every so often I need to swallow my pride and just do it first. A sorry accompanied with a tender hug is even better.

The third rule of engagement is to have the philosophy in marriage that I might not always be right. This is not an easy rule to follow. Our current President of the United States, Donald Trump, recently was quoted saying, "It is amazing how often I am right." That is not a surprising statement coming from him. But when we look at ourselves, we probably unconsciously conduct our own lives with the same philosophy. We most often feel our opinions are the correct ones.

As a type A personality, being open to admitting I am wrong is especially difficult. But most likely our spouses have ideas that have merit. I have learned through experience that this is true more often than I have thought.

We redecorated our house a few years ago with new carpet, paint, and some furniture. There was a place on a large section of the wall that was reserved for multiple pictures of the family to be placed. I had seen in a magazine an example where the pictures were set in different random colored frames and sizes and placed in no particular pattern in the space on the wall. I thought it looked nice but Tonya had different ideas.

She felt the pictures should be all in the same matted black frames and placed in a pattern that was inside a large square section of the space. She wanted it much more uniform and orderly.

Since I was the one doing the work I did it my way. I worked on it for hours finding all the photos and random frames. Then I hammered all the nails into the wall and placed the frames perfectly so that there was nothing ajar. After hours of work Tonya came downstairs to see my work. She said, "That doesn't look good at all." My face got a little steamy after spending so much time on my work of art. I couldn't believe she would say that. I was mad inside but held it in. She left the room and I was ticked off. I just sat there and said, "Now what?"

After a few minutes of staring at the wall, I said to myself, "That does look pretty bad." It could look so much better. I could see it was an area that had potential for so much more. All I could think about was how much time I wasted. All that effort was for nothing. What a disaster.

With my tail between my legs I began to take everything down. Once all the pictures were off the wall, all I could see were the nail holes that needed to be covered. That would be fun.

After going back to the store to buy new frames I started all over again. This time I completed it exactly how Tonya had suggested from the beginning. I had it all placed inside an area of an invisible box and also had all the same colored frames. It looked really good. I sat back and said Tonya was right. When she came down to see for herself there was a smile on her face.

In our marriage, my opinion has been wrong many times. I typically discover this after the fact, versus initially. But the longer I have known Tonya, the more I realize that it is important to get her opinion on decisions. Things typically turn out better that way. I will not buy many clothes without getting the nod from her first. I will not plan vacations without her input. Often when I am making tough decisions, I get her feedback first. Sometimes it is a pain because we disagree and have to work through it. But this is one of the great benefits of marriage: getting each other's views on things to balance our thoughts before making decisions.

Therefore in an argument when we disagree on things, it's important to always have in the back of our minds that there is a slight possibility that we are wrong. Our spouse may be totally in the right. So I don't go to the sheets trying to defend every last element. I realize it may come back to bite me.

Find Something You Both Enjoy Doing Together

It was our 15th wedding anniversary trip to Bora Bora. This island had always been on my bucket list for a romantic beach vacation. It did not disappoint. The over-the-water-bungalows, the view of the island, the wonderful food, and the abundance of sun were an anniversary dream.

Upon arriving, I couldn't keep my eyes off the island's beautiful mountain peak. It was so picturesque on the other side of the ocean bay. The shallow water was a sparkling aqua blue color, filled with all sorts of marine life. The stingrays and many other colorful fish that swam by made it seem like a giant beautiful fish bowl. The mountain was jagged and jungle-like which seemed a perfect place for King Kong to live. I had never seen a more gorgeous beach scene.

After a couple of days of looking at the island, I told Tonya that I wanted to hike to the top of that thing. It seemed like such a challenge. What an adventure it would be. To say I had reached the top would really mean something. Tonya agreed.

I went to the hotel desk and asked if there was an excursion that would take us there. Luckily, it listed an option for a private guide to escort us up the mountain. It was labeled a difficult hike, which didn't bother us, because we were in good shape and had hiked together numerous times.

Tonya and I have loved hiking together ever since our honeymoon in Hawaii where we had an epic 8-mile hike along the Na Pali Coast. We enjoy the exercise, the long conversations, and the beautiful scenes that sometimes can only be seen from a trail. Over time, we have been lucky to see many of the great vistas of the world.

We anticipated another epic vista from the top of this island's beautiful mountain peak. We booked the all day trip for the next day. We were to arrive early at around 8am to take the boat from the outer island, where the hotel was located, to the main island where only locals live. There we were to meet our guide.

The day came and we arrived on the island and met our guide for the day. He was a divorced man in his late 40's who had lived a hard adventurous life. He was originally from South Africa but had lived all over the world. He had always been an adventure guide. The clear plastic sandals he wore intrigued me. I assumed he would be changing into his hiking shoes once we arrived at the starting point.

He began discussing the hike. He said this is very difficult. It would be literally a 35% to 45% grade the whole time. That seemed quite steep. He pointed out that due to the wet slick tree roots and the mud, hiking boots were the worst footwear for the climb. His sandals looked like something one would purchase for 10 dollars at Walmart, but he said they were ideal for the slippery conditions of the mountains.

He placed harnesses on our waists because at times we would be attached to him with ropes for safety. Also, there would be certain spots where it would require ropes to climb up the trail. I thought to myself, 'This will not be some ordinary hike.'

We began the trek. It was a steady climb, as he occasionally whacked the jungle that was ahead of us with his machete. It was rather warm and sticky from the heat and humidity of the island. I quickly got the sense that it was rare for a tourist to take this excursion.

We came to our first rock face that needed to be climbed. It was about 15 feet high. He went first, and then he sent a rope down for us. We hooked it in our harness and then he attached it to him. He was our tree, our security safety, if we fell. Tonya, as always, went first and had no difficulty rock climbing her way up to him. I followed. This hike was just beginning to get interesting.

We continued hiking through the forest at 35% grade for what seemed about an hour, occasionally hitting rock faces that required ropes. We finally reached a vista and a level section where we sat and had lunch and viewed our progress. Within ¾ a mile we had climbed 1500 feet up.

After lunch we headed to the summit. Actually the summit's surface is so loose and steep that no one has ever climbed it. We were headed to a peak just below the summit. As we followed the trail along the mountain it then turned to what seemed straight up. This was the 45% grade section. There were ropes along the trail so that we could scale to the top.

This was the first time on the hike it got scary. Basically if we slipped and fell, the only thing between us and tumbling to our death was our guide. We were attached to him by a rope and nothing else.

Our guide went ahead of us by a few feet. Then, he gathered his footing and had us climb a few feet using the main rope of the trail to hold and walk up. Almost like repelling, but walking up versus down.

We made it up the last 500 feet to the top. We had climbed over 2000 feet in a little over a mile of hiking. The 3-hour trip had been quite the adventure so far, but was a little disappointing at the top. The clouds had moved in and we could hardly see anything. It was like standing in the midst of fog. As we waited, occasionally we could see a little bit of the ocean below. We could barely see our resort through the mist. It was so far away it looked like a little dot on a map.

After some light snacks we decided to head down. Our guide said this is where we had to be careful. I thought to myself, "Oh Boy?" I then looked down the path we had just come up. The 45% looked more like 90% is certain spots. We basically repelled down but unlike normal repelling we were tethered to him versus something stationary. Sometimes he was below us which a fall could have meant 20 or more feet of falling before him possibly stopping us. So we basically had a single long rope to just hold onto. It was all based on our hands to keep us from falling as we leaned back with our feet against the wall or path.

Our guide explained the form to use and Tonya caught on very quickly. She managed one section at a time, while I had more problems. Our guide started to get frustrated with me when I didn't lean back far enough. As we inched down, he gained more and more respect for Tonya and less and less for me. My nerves had gotten the best of me.

Then things got worse. Rain came over the mountain with no warning. Now we had dirt turning slick and muddy. The skies opened up like a monsoon and began to pour buckets of rain. We were drenched immediately.

We finally made it down the steepest section and had a somewhat level path for a bit. Our guide stayed tethered to us just in case we slipped off the path with the rainy conditions. Within minutes that is exactly what happened. I was walking along, then without warning my right foot slipped in the mud and I went tumbling down into the jungle foliage like in a scene from "Romancing the Stone." Luckily, the rope stopped me before I got really hurt. My pride was what got damaged the most from the fall. From there on it was almost like Tonya and our guide were watching out for poor Dave to not hurt himself. Humility?

We made it most of the way down the mountain to the final rope section which was a 15 foot drop. Our guide attached his rope to our harness and held on tight, which anchored us as we repelled down the short drop. He braced himself by placing his front foot on the backside of a tree root to hold all of our weight. I went first and made it down easily.

Tonya was next. She was lighter, which would be less strain for our guide. As she began to repel down, our guide's foot slipped on the wet root. He was the only person supporting her repel. So as his foot slipped in between the roots, her weight caused his leg to get caught between the limbs so that it was on the edge of snapping his tibia and fibula in two. Instinctively, he let himself begin to fall to relieve his leg. Tonya began falling down the wall, which caused him to flip downward over the wall. As he front flipped head first into the air, dislodging his foot from the log, he completed the turn and reached up with one hand to grab a root. His body jerked to a stop as he held on desperately with all his might. His veins in his sweaty arms were popping with Tonya's and his weight pulling him downward. He was able to hold on which stopped Tonya's fall just 3 feet before hitting the ground.

As Tonya was dangling there safely just feet from the ground, I looked up at the guide struggling mightily to hang onto the root keeping her safe. It was the most instinctive and impressive athletic move I had ever seen. Had he just done this? To keep from breaking his leg he had let go, completely flipped over down the wall, yet he caught himself with one hand while supporting Tonya's weight. I yelled, "Amazing, you just saved Tonya's life."

We made it down the final section and gave each other high fives for such an epic, crazy, adventurous day. I tipped him in Francs a large amount that I couldn't even calculate at the time. He smiled because it was more than he expected. To me, he deserved it.

We made it back to our over-the-water bungalow after the sun had gone down and dark had settled in with a full moon shining above. We were more tired than we had ever been before from a hike. We had dirt and mud caked all over us. We could not even walk into our place because we feared tracking in mud.

So I climbed down the ladder and washed off in the 4 feet of ocean water that our bungalow was built over. While rubbing the dirt off my clothes and splashing around to clean up, Tonya yelled down from the deck above, "Don't move!" I immediately stopped cleaning myself and stood nervously wondering what was up. In the moonlight, I couldn't see into the water from where I was standing, so I was relieved when Tonya said, "It's ok now."

I asked her what it was. She said that it was one of the biggest eel shaped creatures she had ever seen. She said it was around two feet in diameter and over 10 feet long as it swam like a snake right by me. I am so glad I didn't see it myself. That image would have stuck with me for a while.

We went to bed that night totally exhausted and sore. We laid there amazed at what we had just done. It was the hardest hike we had ever taken before and the hardest hike since. We said to each other, "who does this sort of thing?" We had to have been crazy to do this on our relaxing anniversary beach vacation to Bora Bora.

Yes, we hiked up that mountain. Not a normal thing to do on a vacation in paradise.

If we were asked, I don't know if we would do that hike all over again. But Tonya and I have found that we really love to hike together. We have found something to do together that we both enjoy. Because of this, we have hiked the world. We have seen most of the National Parks the United States has to offer. We have hiked Canada, Switzerland, Austria, Italy, Hawaii, Norway, and much more. I feel lucky to have a spouse to enjoy hiking with. It is something that enriches our marriage. It is something for us to look forward to in our future. It is something that helps keep our marriage alive and healthy.

However, as our marriage has progressed over time, I have found that there are many things I enjoy doing that are completely independent of Tonya. But because we have found mutual interest in many areas, this has kept our relationship vibrant. We are not completely reliant on our children to entertain us. We have found in a happy marriage we seek to complement each other's differences, as well as develop and grow our similarities. Felix Adler once said, "Love is the expansion of two natures in such a fashion that each include the other, each is enriched by the other. Love is an echo in the feelings of a unity subsisting between two persons, which is founded both on likeness and on complementary differences. Without the likeness there would be no attraction; without the challenge of the complementary differences there could not be the closer interweaving and the inextinguishable mutual interest which is the characteristic of all deeper relationships."

To conclude, three ideas that enhance a marriage relationship are dating, managing disagreements, and finding something that we both enjoy doing together. These are not all it takes to thrive in marriage, but I feel these are a good start. Creating a forever relationship requires a lot of effort. But it is so worth it. Almost all the joys in my life have had my marriage center pieced right in the middle of them.

Questions to consider: How am I creating more love in my life? If married, what do I do to work on my relationship?

CHAPTER 7

My Philosophy On Money

"People think about money more than anything else in their life." –Mike Ertz

I stirred and stirred to get the bigger clumps out. Chocolate pudding always tastes better smooth. As I wiped around the top edges of the bowl to get every last bit of dry powder into the mix, I imagined that first bite going down. Instant pudding has always been such an easy and cheap way to finish off a meal.

I stuck my finger in the mix to test it out. "Perfect." Just how I liked it. I went to get the bowls so we could eat some right away. As I grabbed the bowls from the cabinet and turned to walk back to fill them up I was greeted with a glob of pudding right between the eyes. I was stunned. Tonya had snuck into our little apartment kitchen area and had decided it was time for a food fight. After the shock, a big smile broke out on my face. Dripping down my nose was some of the best tasting brown pudding. It was go time.

I reached for the bowl and grabbed a handful. My first attempt was a forehead shot. It was a direct hit. After that, mayhem broke out. As we laughed and laughed we began smearing it into each other's face and hair. Running away was no use. Soon, it was in our nose and ears. Our hair was filled with large chunks and it was all over our clothes. Pudding was splattered on the walls, floor and cabinets. It looked like mud was everywhere. We found ourselves quite talented in creating a quick mess.

Finally, we ran out of pudding. When we stopped, we laughed as we looked at each other's slimy faces. Being newlyweds we didn't clean up immediately, instead we supposed it to be a perfect time to finish this off with a messy make out session. The evening was just getting started. Married life has its perks. I loved it!

Pudding fight in our first year of marriage.

In our first year of marriage we had little money but it was one of the best periods of our lives. We spent time together, with most evenings and weekends to ourselves. The type of fun we had had nothing to do with money. Think about it, the average cost of a mix of pudding was less than a dollar.

We paid for most of our wedding ourselves, which made our first year of marriage an interesting financial time. We had traveled to Utah to get married and then went to Hawaii for our honeymoon. We loved the great memories it created, but it was not cheap. This was the beginning of my learning an important lesson about money.

It all started with a little moment of stress on the honeymoon. While walking on a Kauai beach, stress began to build in my mind when I tried to estimate the real cost of the wedding. I was realizing that after everything we had paid, we probably still accrued $5,000 of credit card debt. That thought just frightened me. I said to myself, "I hope I have just miscalculated." That was my method to stay mentally happy while celebrating our honeymoon.

Upon arriving home from the trip, crunching the numbers, I found I had miscalculated. We owed $10,000. When I saw this number, I felt a lump in my throat and a pit in my stomach. That was huge. How could this have happened? How would I get out of this? I was being paid commission in my new business and had a small, sporadic income. I felt overwhelmed. This is how financial stress feels. It's horrible.

I had never had credit card debt before, nor have I since. That year, it became our main goal to get back on track as soon as possible. The stress of debt was pervasive throughout much of the first year of our marriage. We were having a great time as newlyweds but the debt was always on my mind. Luckily, I was blessed to have a wife on the same financial page. We worked on this together. I learned pretty quickly that financial stress is one of the worst kinds of stress. There is a reason it is the number one cause for divorce in America. It creates heaviness in the mind that is hard to relieve.

With a lot of hard work, good budgeting, and some good fortune, we had it paid off in 10 months. From this experience I have made some observations regarding money that can dramatically impact happiness and success in life. Understanding money is so important. It is a big part of our lives. Therefore, I feel it is a mistake not to understand it and have philosophies around it.

I was blessed to learn most of what I know about money and self-reliance from my father. I have watched how he viewed and handled money. He didn't talk about it much but seeing him live it was quite an education.

He grew up in a small logging community along the Columbia River in the state of Washington. His parents were very simple in their lifestyle. They had steady work but the hourly pay wasn't much. My dad made more than his father while working on a tugboat in high school.

After high school, my dad left the small town to pursue his girlfriend who was attending BYU in Utah. This was almost a thousand miles away and was a big leap for him. He went to Utah with very little money to his name. He would not get any financial help from his parents.

Within months his girlfriend broke up with him. He was left in Utah with nothing but himself and an opportunity for an education. Fortunately, he decided to stay. His college education was one of the biggest gifts of his life. BYU provided a new perspective to see what was really possible. This was not normal for kids from his small river town. Many of his friends from home would never see in life what my dad was able to see. His college education changed his life.

He did have one problem. He had no money. So he had to figure this out on his own. Of course, he always had a job in college. He lived in the cheapest circumstances possible. He also went deer hunting in the fall so he could live off the venison all winter. He did every creative thing he could think of to make it.

At one point, he was living in the basement of a house off campus with some guys. He heard about someone who had a live lamb for sale at a low cost. He figured this was another cheap way for food in the coming months. So he purchased the lamb and put him in the backyard so he could have a place to stay until the dreaded day.

My father was perplexed on how to kill the lamb. He lived in a neighborhood with houses all around. Fences separated each house but they were so close together in the neighborhood that he figured it would not be legal to shoot a gun. He didn't grow up on a farm, so he had no clue on how to do it. All he could think of was to slit its throat with a knife. That would have to do. Unfortunately, there was no YouTube video to educate him. He had no experience using a knife in this way. He was nervous.

The day came to stop feeding the animal and have it start providing food for him. He went into the backyard with a knife in hand and said, "Ok, here it goes." He found it harder than he thought to capture it and hold it in position. He described the chase in this manner, "With my inexperience, all I could say is when I was done, the backyard had blood and carnage everywhere. It looked like a murder scene of epic proportion. I felt bad for how that lamb had to pass." He said, "Later when the homeowner happened to drop by the house, he saw the scene and was not pleased with the condition of his backyard. I was lucky he didn't kick me out."

It's difficult to imagine a college student today having this experience. If it were posted on Instagram he would have all sorts of trouble. Protestors of all types would have something to say. But in my father's day, he just did what he had to do to survive with the little resources he had. My college experience sure differed from his.

Food for the next 4 months of college.

But this is something we could all learn from. My father did everything he could to rely on himself. He was forced to. He learned this at an early age and never looked back. He taught me how important it is to own your financial situation. We all have bad breaks, but we need to learn to own it and figure out a way to get through.

Our society is filled with examples of people blaming others for their circumstances. In certain situations it may even be reasonable to feel that way. But casting blame will not help the situation. Not assigning blame is the first step to being self-reliant. And self-reliance is the first step to feeling free. Sukarno said, " We feel free... Now we are really self-reliant. This is the great advantage of teaching ourselves to become a free person, no longer one that always asks, "Aid, aid, please."

I have done financial planning for the past 26 years. I have met with thousands of people to discuss their financial plans. I don't know if I have seen it all, but it is rare that I see anything new. I have observed that there are basic principles everyone should strive for. I have seen clients who followed these principles, feel secure, not just at retirement, but throughout their lives.

The first principle, and maybe the most important, is to live on less than we make. Staying out of debt is the key! I know that we have heard this over and over but most people still don't do this. According to the Nerdwallet's study, "The average 2018 American household's revolving debt is $6,829. This is typically at interest rates of 18-21%. Our lifestyles can get out of control. Credit cards are sneaky with all the deals that are available. They lure us to use them. Because of this, families with credit card debt have so much more financial stress than those that don't. I have seen families with 200k plus incomes with 50k of credit card debt. Even with nice careers, they are in financial prison.

I use credit cards all the time. I just pay them off every month with no interest. I benefit from them by getting free miles for flights. It saves us money every year, with our travels. But I continue to remind myself: with cards someone is always earning interest. We don't want to let the credit card companies earn from us; we ought to be the ones earning.

I have found there are only three things that are legitimate purposes for debt.

1. A reasonable house

2. A reasonable car

3. A reasonable college education.

Other than that, we should pay cash for everything. I advise clients: Don't buy it unless you can pay for it now. I use the word "reasonable" for house, car, and education costs, because in all three of those areas I have seen situations where they have crippled a family's financial freedom. The best advice is not to become "house poor" where a huge mortgage eats up any discretionary spending.

The second principle around money I can illustrate with an experience. When Tonya and I had been married about five years I had a bad six months in my business. We made very little commission during that time and we started to hurt. For most of our marriage we had been getting by and making it without budgeting.

I have heard that if we budgeted we could probably live on half of what our normal discretionary spending is for each month. There are fixed bills, like the mortgage payment, that we pay in the same amount every month. Then there are discretionary bills like groceries, supplies, restaurants, gas, and fun. These are expenses that fluctuate according to personal decisions made each month. It's in the discretionary spending that we can make a financially positive impact immediately.

To stick to a budget, we were simplistic in our approach. We put a piece of paper on the counter in the main area of the kitchen. We wrote on the top of the sheet five categories, ranging from groceries to entertainment. We placed the dollar amount we could spend in each category for that month. We used numbers that were half of what was spent in previous months. On a daily basis, we wrote down anything we spent in real time and refigured how much money was left to spend for the month. Consequently, we always knew where we were. Amazingly, we reached our goal month after month and spent half of the norm.

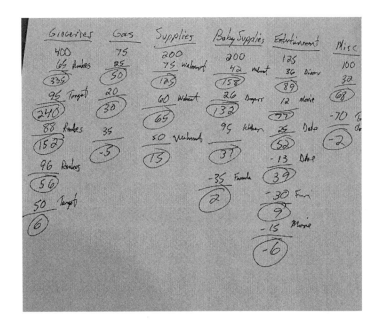

Sample month of our budgeting worksheet. Very basic.

The other interesting discovery was that we didn't change our lifestyle much. It didn't feel different. We still went on dates. We still spent time together having fun. We just didn't spend as much money doing it. We didn't spend it casually. Every dollar counted. Steve Jobs is known to have said, "My favorite things in life didn't cost any money. It's really clear that the most precious resource we all have is time."

There are so many digital tools to help. But most of them are based on end-of-month numbers that we can analyze to do better the next month. This is helpful but not as useful as it needs to be. Our simple piece of paper was what we needed. We were reminded of it every time we walked into the kitchen. It only took a second to write it down. Those who use a program will want to make sure it is quick to input and is a system that is in real time so that throughout the month they can know exactly how much money they have left. And of course it is wise to make it one that both spouses can see. Today a phone could be used as effectively, as long as a reminder is set every day to remind you to input expenses.

A third principle to financial security is to have four different buckets of money to save and invest over time. Most people want to diversify risk with investing. But few people diversify the purpose of their investments. To illustrate this, I once met a 50-year-old successful executive who was making a 6-digit income and had accumulated 4 million dollars in his retirement accounts. Most people would look at him as financially secure and rich. But when I met him he was stressed out of his mind. He had two kids in college and had not saved for it. The schools they chose were expensive and he had committed to his children to pay for their education. His retirement accounts would incur major penalties and taxes if he tapped into them. So he was paying for college out of income and some loans. His budget and lifestyle were strained at one of the highest income periods of his life. He had all of his money wrapped up in the retirement bucket. He may have the capacity to feel secure once he retires but he sure didn't feel financial security at age 50.

I want my clients to feel secure throughout their lives, not just retirement. To do this, I suggest they allocate the money they are putting away for the future into four different buckets. They are all equally important.

The first bucket is to have three months to six months of one's after tax income in the bank for emergencies. The return on investment is not the main concern here. It is safety and liquidity that is paramount. This is not a checking account from which bills are paid. This is money set aside that is sacred and not to be touched, except for true emergencies. Such an emergency might be the death of a family member and the resulting need to fly across the country. This liquid account allows one to have money for the trip and avoids debt. I find this discipline is difficult for many families to keep in place. It's easy to start thinking that everything is an emergency and to tap into the money regularly. I recommend for most to have the money in a place that is out of sight and out of mind.

Bucket number two is to have a short to mid-term mutual fund or stock portfolio. This is invested and will have some level of risk, depending on one's risk tolerance. Long term, it should grow but will have its ups and downs. Long term it will outperform the return of cash. The purpose of the second bucket is to have money for that first house five to 10 years in the future or maybe that next car, or a piece of furniture. This is a bucket some clients rarely touch and it grows to substantial amounts in the future. I have found that when clients have money in this bucket, it creates an added feeling of financial security. It is almost like a second emergency account because it can be cashed in at any time.

The third bucket is mid to long-term money. These are dollars that can be spent before and during retirement but are meant for 15 to 20 years down the road. According to current tax law, this money is also tax favorable in some way. Otherwise we would just put it all into the second bucket. 529 plans for college and cash value from permanent life insurance are the two vehicles we use for this bucket. I have found it nice to have some money built up that when I'm ready to spend it, it could come out of the fund without tax. This has been particularly helpful now that I am in a higher tax bracket in my early 50's.

The fourth bucket is retirement plans. There are many types of plans out there. Employers typically provide either a deductible 401k or a Roth 401k. The first is deductible up front but all the taxes will need to be paid later, at retirement. A Roth is not deductible but will be tax-free later. Both can get a contribution match from an employer, which is free money. I always want to at least max out the match with my contributions. If possible, I like to contribute to the limits the IRS allows. Ideally I would contribute so that I end up with half my retirement taxable and half of my retirement tax-free. That way we can manage our tax bracket when we retire, which can potentially save thousands of dollars a year.

When clients have these four buckets and appropriate debt, I have noticed they are secure in all of their stages of life. This doesn't require someone to be rich. It is relative to their income. They can just feel secure. Now there are many other ways that one might invest money wisely. I have seen people become financially secure with real estate, business ownership, and many other ways; this just seems to be the most helpful to my clients and myself.

I recommend that, regardless of the level of salary, people put away 20% of their gross income. If that is too hard from where they stand, then they can start at a lower percentage and work to increase it from there. When I was young with no kids and I had our wedding debt paid off, we started with 30% because it was a focus early. If a person can build their expenses after their set investing percentage, versus investing whatever is left each month, it will make it so much easier. Because I invested at a higher percentage than needed, now at age 50, I am way ahead and can retire early.

The 4th principle I have about money is a game changer. I have always done this and it has helped me emotionally deal with money more than anything else. I will describe this principle with an experience.

When I graduated from college I decided to go into the same line of business as my father. He managed a life insurance firm in Cincinnati and had become very successful. I saw that path as doable since he had set the vision. I decided life insurance sales would be my specialty. About 10% of those who start in this field are still there 5 years later. I knew it must be hard, but I figured if I could be a successful missionary in Texas I could do about anything. I was naive and not scared.

My father's company did not train new people, so he recommended a different firm to learn the trade. When I got started, they wanted me to have a list of 200 friends that I could begin calling on for sales and referrals. I had grown up out west and was new to the Cincinnati area. I came up with 30 people and they were mainly people my parents knew from church. I started out with a major disadvantage.

At the very beginning of training, we were told that we would need to make 30 phone calls daily. I thought to myself, "If that's the case, with my 30 names I only have one day of work." So when I called people from my list, my focus was to get referrals right away. My first two appointments happened to be with good friends of my parents. They each generously gave me 15 referrals. Now I had 58 people left to call. A light bulb went off in my head.

I started to get the hang of the activity that was needed to be successful. Unfortunately, I still wasn't making many sales and certainly not much money. My sales skills were just horrible.

After three months, I found a friend of my parents who was a successful executive in his mid forties who had a need for a large amount of life insurance. Even though it was hard to get an appointment, the day finally came where we were able to meet.

After some small talk I began to discuss business. As I went through my basic presentation, he asked me a question to which I did not know the answer. I told him I would need to get back to him on that. Then he asked me another question that I didn't know. I again said that I would need to get back with him. He got frustrated with me and said, "David, you are a bad salesperson." My mind began to race inside. What a bold statement to say. His statement really stung. I felt a good rapport with him but that rapport was not enough to compensate for a lack of knowledge and professionalism. I did not get the sale, and I walked out completely depressed and blown away. I said to myself, "You are a bad salesperson? No one will ever say that to me again."

As I drove home, I was half mad from his comment and I was half sad because of another failure in my career. The sadness took over and all I could feel was a big lump in my throat. I felt broken from it all. I had just had another really bad day. Not too different than many others. I thought to myself, when is it going to get better? This business was so hard. It wore on my soul.

I decided to add up roughly how many hours I had worked in the first three months; then I added up the gross commissions I had been paid. I thought it would be interesting to find my hourly rate. That was a mistake. My calculation was $2.37 per hour. I had made more working at McDonald's in college.

At that moment I felt totally poor with no end in sight. The stress and anxiety was peaking at that moment until I began to pray. This was not a kneel down beside my bed kind of prayer. It was a depressed, driving down the road, kind of prayer that I spoke out loud to God. I asked Him, "Where are you?" After speaking my peace to God for a minute, I felt the Spirit directing a thought to my head. What the Spirit spoke to my soul that day changed my view about money forever. He said, "You are a full tithe payer. It will all work out." At that moment I had a calm feeling come over me. My worry about money, my business, and my future all dissipated. I knew that in time, somehow and in some way it would all work out. I just needed to keep learning and growing until I could be successful.

In our church we follow the Biblical principle of giving 10% of our gross income to the church. Thanks to my parents, I have been faithful in this principle since I was a child. During this period of my life my $2.37 per hour was not much money but I still paid my tithing during that time. There is a scripture in the Old Testament Malachi 3:10-11 that says, "Bring ye all the tithes into the storehouse, that there may be meat in mine house, and prove me now herewith, saith the Lord of hosts, if I will not open you the windows of heaven, and pour you out a blessing, that there shall not be room enough to receive it. And I will rebuke the devourer for your sakes, and he shall not destroy the fruits of your ground; neither shall your vine cast her fruit before the time in the field, saith the Lord of hosts."

It was the time in my life for God to prove it to me. This was my day. It was my moment. Even though it would take a couple years to feel truly stable, at that moment, I had a calm feeling of confidence that I knew I could do it, and that God was going to help me. What a strategic advantage in business! Confidence is a top indicator of success. My confidence came from God. What better confidence can we get than that?

This was a big moment for me. It sticks out as a great learning experience as it relates to money. I learned that if you want to have confidence with money BE GENEROUS WITH IT. For some, it may be tithing along with giving to other worthy causes. For others, generous giving may be completely independent from a religion. Regardless, the principle applies. What we give away with pure intent comes back to us in some form or another. We may not be rich because of it, but we will have our needs met.

I have seen it over and over again. What is so comforting is when a generous person has a moment of weakness in his financial picture; he or she can have faith that things will work out. I have found this to be a reliable principle, one that creates the confidence to move forward. Some might call it karma or good luck. I call it a God's blessing on generosity. All I know is that it is a true principle.

Finally in 1995 I moved out of the cubicles and into my first personal office at Northwestern Mutual. It was small with no windows, but I was proud of it.

My fifth principle about money is to pick the right career. This is a tricky choice, because careers are multifaceted and it's hard to discern how one's own skill set might fit a certain career path.

Additionally, not all careers pay the same. In choosing a career, it's wise to keep in mind the statement from Bob Dylan, "What's money? A man is a success if he gets up in the morning and goes to bed at night and in between does what he wants to do." That means that while our career choices need to provide enough to support a lifestyle, it is equally important that the work is something that is personally meaningful and enjoyable.

I think most people feel that money should be the primary consideration with the career choice they make. It's a common thought that the more income one has, the happier he will be. But experience shows this isn't always the case. In fact, a study conducted by Princeton economist Angus Deaton and famed psychologist Daniel Kahneman showed in 2010 that the income needed to create peak happiness for a family was $75,000 per year. In the economy of 2020, that would translate to approximately $87,000, which is an above-average income in American today, but it does not fall into the ultra wealthy category as people might expect. There seems to be a bell curve in which the poor do not have enough of their basic needs met to experience "peak happiness" and the ultra wealthy have so much that they have a hard time not being distracted from what truly creates happiness.

The study seems to indicate that perhaps the things acquired with dollars above $87,000 become just more stuff in our lives. Perhaps excess can dull the desire to be challenged at work. Perhaps we get trapped in jobs that require all our time in order to make that amount of money. Perhaps the overall situation of the poor and the rich have similarities, it makes it difficult to dedicate enough time and energy to our relationships that matter most.

Of course there are many exceptions to this with the poor and the rich. We can all rise above our circumstances. But the probability of happiness is higher when your income is around $87,000, so when choosing a career it's wise to keep the bell curve in mind and refrain from choosing a career just because it seems to offer the best income.

There are three types of work that people do. Some people have a job, some people have a career, and some people have a passion for which they get paid. All types are admirable and can facilitate a happy life. All three can create financial security, as I described earlier in this chapter. All three types of work can allow a person to practice generosity.

The first, those who have a job, are those individuals who work for an organization and put in a hard days work. They support their family and can be very happy in life. They typically get paid for the skills and training that they have. Hopefully they enjoy doing their work most of the time. They often want as many vacation days as possible and look forward for the day to be over so they can get home to put up their feet and relax. They dream of retirement and are content with their current position at work. Climbing the corporate ladder is not a goal.

My ancestry is part Norwegian; and in my travels to Norway I discovered that their society is driven by a flat business system of contentment. They all have a job, 8 weeks of vacation, and they don't view their boss as any more fortunate than they are. They each have a job and a role to play. They don't worry much about college education, medical costs, or retirement. They are all taken care of by the government from the heavy tax base they are accessed. It has created a flat business system without much rich or poor. This Norwegian system perpetuates having jobs, not careers or passions.

The second type of work is what I call a career. This kind of work is most likely to be found in a capitalistic system where free markets flourish. Places like America, where one can come from a limited background and grow his or her resources into something of significance. I put myself in this category. I started my career making $2.37 an hour and eventually developed a financial planning firm that helps many families, including some of the wealthiest in my community and across the country.

A career is a type of labor that requires growth and expansion. Whether it is growing one's business or finding ways to add notable professional value to a corporation. Careers can involve personal risk, investment of time, financial outlay, and complicated decisions. However, the planning, the education and the investments of time and money early in a career can mature into expertise that deserves compensation and that results in a very generous lifestyle over time. Some primary drivers for choosing a career over a job might involve the opportunities to grow personally, to make an impact, and to enhance one's income.

The last type of work might be best described as finding a career that is a joy, a passion, and sometimes a cause. People who find themselves in a career they value this highly have been known to say that they would do their work for free. It might be a professional basketball player who loves playing ball. It might be a scientist who works 80 hours a week to find a cure to a worldwide disease. It might be a high school drama teacher who loves the youth and has a passion for theater. These people are often the best in their field. They love their work. They have a passion for it. They could work 90 hours a week and love every minute of it. These are men and women who can't wait to get back from vacation because they know they get to return to work. Often these people can make large sums of money if the career provides it, but money is not their goal, it is only the byproduct of quality, hard work.

Typically this type of career has its pros and cons. The pros are: their work feels important to them, their successes impact themselves and others in a significant way, they feel they are one of the only persons capable of doing what they can do. Typically financial results can be high.

The cons can be that people with such a passion for their career might lack some balance in their lives. They might overlook the blessing of devoting time to other priorities, like family, friends, and faith. I have always believed that TIME=PRIORITIES. Therefore, some things can take a second seat to the bigger issues. We have all seen driven individuals who are at the top of their fields but have a wreck of a home life.

It takes a special person to be passionate for career and family life too. My father was a good example of this. He didn't miss many races of mine when I was in school. He did a good job spending time with family and friends. But he also had a deep passion for his work. In year-end speeches it was normal for him to tear up, speaking to colleagues about the insurance business. His extreme passion just bled out of his every pore. He absolutely loved it. Today, in his mid 70's, most mornings he can be found in his home study, reading insurance business journals or calling on the wealthy to help them buy the protection of life insurance. It is in his blood.

Most people consider me a very successful business owner. I enjoy what I do. There are many aspects about it that perfectly fit my personality. I love how I can make a difference to my client's lives. But rarely do I tear up. Rarely at this stage of my life do I work over 40 hours a week. I can only imagine that if it were my passion, my revenue might be many multiples of the current amounts.

As young people enter the career world, I encourage them to decide on what is most important. All three types of work can create happiness. Those that are aligned with what is most important to them are the ones that will be most happy, and the commensurate financials will follow.

The sixth principle about money considers the way to think about money. Or what our philosophy of money should be. Benjamin Franklin alluded to one philosophy, when he said, "Money has never made man happy, nor will it, there is nothing in its nature to produce happiness. The more of it one has, the more one wants." I completely agree with this. Whenever I buy things, I am excited at first, but the excitement is fleeting. I've learned the truth of Franklin's comment: buying things will not solve a person's lack of happiness.

My philosophy about money is that wealth is neither good nor bad. It simply enhances or magnifies the character of the person who has it. I have seen wealth turn bad people into worse people by giving them fuel for their destructive behavior.

I have also seen wealth give good people much greater capacity to do even more good. They have used their wealth to change their family, friends, and society for the better. They have been able to use their time differently for the service of others because of financial independence. Their wealth is a great enhancer.

Now having said this, the more money one has, the more careful he or she needs to be to not let it change them. We all have a propensity for "the love of money," which, according to scripture can be the beginning or the "the root of all evil." The love of money and the love of more and more things is not good. Its pursuit often gives us unhealthy freedoms and the capacity to get into negative circumstances. Money simply supplies more options, freedom, flexibility, and time. These things can get us in trouble. Matthew McConaughey said, "Too many options makes a tyrant out of all of us."

I believe God cares about our self-reliance but he is not impressed with how much money we make and the amount of our net worth. He looks to our hearts, not pocketbooks. As we look at our friends and acquaintances it might be important to follow God's example. It would be interesting to audit who our closest friends are, to see if all of them are only in a certain financial situation. It seems like it would be healthy to have a wide financial spectrum among those with whom we spend time. I have seen some of the best people in this world come from all levels of income. A mentor once told me: "Remember, money is neutral. Don't let it be anything but that in your life."

Questions to consider: Am I taking the proper steps to be financially secure? Are my friends only those in the same social economic situation that I am in?

CHAPTER 8

Raising a Family

"Listen to your life. See it for the fathomless mystery that it is...Touch, taste, smell your way to the holy and hidden heart of it because in the last analysis all moments are key moments, and life itself is grace." –Frederick Buechner

Tonya yelled from the kitchen, "David, you better come here quick." I ran to see what was the matter. She did not often have that sound in her voice. She looked at me with an amazed stare as she stood in the middle of a clear watery puddle. In a somber voice she said, "My water broke." My brain immediately started to ponder. Does this mean it is really happening? The baby wasn't supposed to come for two more weeks. Does it all start with this? The whole process was new to us. We had just come home from church and had plans for dinner with the family. Those plans were now changed. We were headed for the hospital!

I was not fully prepared for what happens when a mother gives birth. I watched Tonya endure for hours the immense pain and struggle that came with delivering our baby boy. I was impressed by her focus and determination to get through it without medication. There was a great sense of relief when our son finally came out healthy and strong. As my wife lay there totally exhausted from 17 hours of struggle, it surprised me to see the scene of carnage from the delivery. She was ripped and torn with a cord hanging out of her. Blood and fluids were everywhere. Her body had been through so much. I said to myself, "I can't believe this is the way a baby is born. Does everyone go through this? How could this be natural?"

The doctor stitched her back together as she laid there with Ethan snuggled up to her breast. The exhausted proud smile on her face was the look of the complete mother. Our son, on the other hand, looked like a slimy cone-headed character from Saturday Night Live. His eyes were like black marbles peering through puffy Asian eyes. He was pooping out bizarre black charcoal waste. I just never expected this. I had never seen that before. Welcome to fatherhood.

The nurses were soon poking and pricking him with shot after shot. I felt sorry for the little guy. I thought to myself, "Ouch, that would hurt." Then, later that day came the circumcision. Now that was a whole new kind of hurt. I just cringed thinking of what he was about to experience. I was thankful he would not remember it.

For me, the whole hospital sequence was like a startling amusement park ride. I was on it and I had signed up for it, but had my hair standing on end at every corner.

The first night at home was when parenting really began. We were up most of the night trying to keep him fed and comfortable. It wasn't automatic for Tonya and the baby to breastfeed. Tonya struggled through it until it became normal. I marveled at how helpless and tiny Ethan was. He needed us for everything to survive. He would literally die within days without our attention.

The thought came to my mind, "Where is the manual for all of this?" This is serious stuff. How are we going to get this right? How are we going to keep him alive? How will we raise our son to be happy, healthy, and loving person? I had heard all of the quotes. Jane Dee Hull once said, "At the end of the day, the most overwhelming key to a child's success is the positive involvement of parents." So how do we positively stay involved? David O. McKay also said, "No other success can compensate for failure in the home." So what do we need to do not to fail? Jeffrey Holland said, "Our children take their flight into the future with our thrust and with our aim. And even as we anxiously watch that arrow in flight and know all the evils that can deflect its course after it has left our hand, nevertheless, we take courage in remembering that the most important mortal factor in determining that arrow's destination will be the stability, strength, and unwavering certainty of the holder of the bow." So how can we be the stable and strong constant in his life? Wow, all of this is almost too much for the new parent to take in!

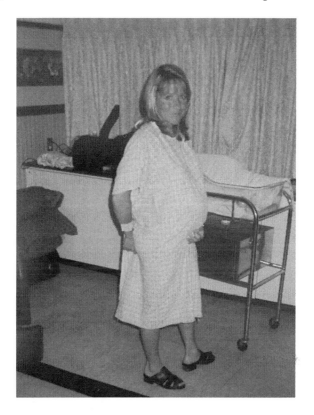

At the hospital before the delivery of our first child Ethan.

Two weeks after Ethan was born, we had some friends over to the house. They asked me what I thought of parenting so far. Foolishly I responded, "It wasn't as hard as I thought it would be. It's not too bad." Tonya was sitting there holding the baby. Immediately her eyes were fiery mad as she stared into my soul. She couldn't believe I had just said that. I think when a couple has a child, the parent who is the primary caretaker—usually the woman—is exhausted and the other parent can sometimes be totally clueless.

Frankly, I had slept most nights since we had come home from the hospital. Tonya was breastfeeding so I was useless when Ethan was hungry. Occasionally in the night she asked if I could rock him to sleep if he was fussy. But it wasn't often enough to wear me out much. So from my point of view this parent thing was not too bad.

Tonya on the other hand was not complaining but was as tired as could be. I didn't notice it as much as I should have. She was constantly stressed, wondering if the baby was all right. Her breasts were sore. She didn't have family around to help after the first couple days. She woke up at the smallest of noises from the baby monitor. She was struggling with no routine, just reacting to every last need of our new child.

When she did have some free time, she read everything that she could get her hands on that provided advice to a new mother. There are no shortages on mothering newborn books. She read every last one of them.

What she learned is that people have their own theories on what works best. There were opposing views in many areas around parenting a newborn. The techniques used were almost like a religion to some, as they felt they knew what worked best. But in all the many views there was one constant that stuck out in every book, "Children thrive on routine."

Newborns don't have much routine at all. Their bodies are changing rapidly and it seems like parents are in reaction mode 24 hour a day. It makes life so hard. We found the first three months in the lives of each of our four children really difficult for us.

After three months, a routine slowly set in. It started with allowing Ethan to cry out one night. We let him cry for an hour and twenty minutes. It was excruciating, listening to him scream that long. I often wondered what made a baby's cry so horrible to listen to. There is just something heart wrenching about it for a parent. Because of this, more than once we were tempted to call it off and settle him down. But we held on and eventually he fell asleep. It was a victory we had won! The next night he cried for 30 minutes and next, less than that. Then a sleeping routine was born.

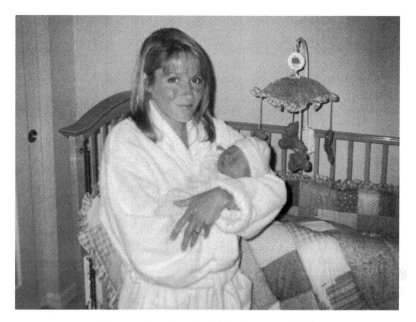

Two weeks after his birth she was a tired momma.

Routine is one of the most important principles in parenting. It is not just for infants. Kids of all ages thrive on routine. In an "Aha Parenting" article I read, "Children, like the rest of us, handle change best if it is expected and occurs in the context of a familiar routine. A predictable routine allows children to feel safe, and to develop a sense of mastery in handling their lives." Jason Selk said, "Rookie coaches are afraid of repetition." Yet it is one of the keys to mastering a sport. It is also a key to children.

As parents, we tried to establish routine in a variety of areas. I will mention three that I feel have been the most important and impactful to our family. It certainly isn't an all-inclusive list. But from my perspective they have played the biggest role in nurturing our kids and being close as a family.

Bedtime Routine

First, we decided from the earliest age possible to have a bedtime routine. This bedtime routine has not changed to this day. Regularly, my teenagers come to me and say, "I am going to bed, so will you come lay with me?" Now that terminology might sound inappropriate to ask a father in that way. But at a very young age our kids said it in that way and it just stuck, without us ever thinking anything of it. Maybe in today's politically correct world, a good substitute would be "Will you come say 'Goodnight,' dad?" However one says it, our kids don't want to go without it. It is one of the best parts of their day. Frankly, it is one of the best parts of mine.

The bedroom routine consists of three things. Tonya and I each participate in the routine separately so each child gets more time, one-on-one. When all four kids were in the home it would take about an hour; around 15 minutes per child. We would lie down next to them and talk, while we gave them a back rub. I typically came into the room and asked, "Legs or back?" What child doesn't want that? They loved to relax before bed. In high school after a tough workout, my boys would often want their leg muscles kneaded, while our girls often preferred a back massage. But whatever they choose, they have learned to appreciate a good massage.

As part of the conversation I have always asked them, "What's the best part of your day?" It gets them talking. I have found, as they lay there relaxed, I often had some of the best conversations of the day. It was enlightening to see what was important to them.

Before saying goodnight I have always included one reason why I love them from that day. I try to pick it from that day's experiences. A typical example might be, "I love you because I noticed you goofing off with your mom today. I think it is so cool how you have such a great relationship with her." I never want my kids to have any doubt that I love them. I want them to know I find new reasons to love them every day. It needs to be more than just words. But words are essential to self-esteem.

To illustrate the importance of our bedtime routine, I want to share an experience with our son Blake. When he was in middle school, he spoke with a lisp. Most of his "S's" sounded like a "Th." He had spoken this way throughout his life, from sucking his thumb for years as a child. It wasn't a huge problem among friends yet, but we thought the older he got the harder it would be for him to fix it.

We found a speech therapist to work with him weekly. She had many things for him to practice at home to improve his sounds. We found that this was not something he liked doing. It was a little awkward for him, and he wasn't good at it. Because of this, he stopped working on the speech disciplines at home. The result was that after taking him to the therapist weekly for 6 months we noticed little to no change in his speech.

Finally, I decided to use our time together right before bed to work on his speech practice. I figured while I was rubbing his back or legs it would take his mind off of what we were doing and it might be more productive. We spent our first 10 minutes of bedtime routine for practice then we put it down and just hung out for a few more minutes before saying goodnight.

This went on for about 2 months. Still there wasn't much progress but the practice was so much more effective because he was mostly in a good, relaxed mood while working on it. Then one day it just happened. He figured it out. He was able to keep his tongue off the back of his upper teeth on his "S's." It was like a miracle. The words that had given him so much trouble now sounded perfect. He was so proud of himself. We celebrated with a lot of high fives that night. We feel correcting his speech issue is one of the bigger gifts we gave Blake growing up.

Had we not had the bedtime routine built in the previous 11 years, we would have most likely never gotten rid of that lisp. It certainly played a large role.

The bedtime routine with our kids has been priceless. Some of the biggest laughs, the deepest conversations, the best teaching moments, the most informative discussions, and some of the most bonding moments with our kids occurred in the last 15 minutes of their day. It has always been one of my favorite times of the day.

Dinner as a Family

Another routine that became important for us is not a new thing, but a valuable one. It was simply to eat dinner together. In today's environment, with parents' working hours and kids' extracurricular schedules it has become more rare to consistently pull off. It is not a unique idea, but it does require intentionality to maintain this routine, even a few nights per week, especially when the kids are in high school.

Eating dinner together has created some great memories for our family. It is also a constant in our kid's lives. Judith Martin said, "The family dinner table is the cornerstone of civilization and those who 'graze' from refrigerators or in front of the television sets are doomed to remain in a state of savagery."

We want this time together to be meaningful. Not just stuffing our faces. To keep the conversation at dinner engaging, we do not allow phones at the table. We also ask a question to each family member, "What is your good and bad for today?" We then listen to the event of the day, which stuck out in their mind as positive. Then we find out what was hard. We do allow them to mention two goods if they don't have a bad. However, we don't allow two bads. We have found this pattern has kept us conversing with each member of the family versus just eating our food and running off to do our own thing. We like the fact that this doesn't feel regimented. It seems to just flow into natural dinner table conversation.

We have not been perfect about the habit of eating together every night. There are nights it is not possible to sit down together. But the majority of nights throughout our kids' lives we have eaten together. Tonya has played a large role by preparing meals throughout the years. This, of course, takes time. Because she does not work outside the home it makes it more possible. I understand how this may feel almost impossible with both spouses working full time jobs. Even with Tonya not working, she needs some breaks from the daily motherly grind. On Friday night we have "Chipotle Night" to give her a day off. On Saturday we have our date night so the kids are on their own. But that ends up being six nights a week that we eat together which certainly establishes a pattern.

Our kid's favorite dinner is a crock-pot slow cooked roast with Tonya's delicious mashed potatoes. It never gets old. This meal seems to be a constant for Sunday dinner. The dinner's aroma in the house when we arrive home from church is something to die for. On Sunday we have our parents and sometimes friends from the church to eat with us.

One day in particular we had Tonya's parents, my mother, and two Christian missionaries over for Sunday dinner. My father-in law Fred is an 80-year-old German who came to America at the age of 12, right after World War II. He only spoke German when he arrived. I can only imagine what the middle school kids said to him to poke fun. He quickly developed a thick skin, going from one fight to another. It would be interesting to think of how Fred would have turned out, had he not met a great woman named Ella at a young age. He loved hanging out at her family's house. They married young. She probably saved him from a very different life.

Fred is the type of guy who would do anything for his family. For years, he was my handyman who helped me with every house issue that would crop up. I love him to death.

But if there is one thing that Fred will always be known for is that he has no filter. As he gets older, it only gets worse and worse. There could be a book compiling his many quotes that could be a bestseller. What's funny is that when you are an 80-year-old German you can get away with anything. If he thinks someone is fat, he will ask them why they are fat. If he hasn't seen you at church, he will ask you the first time he sees you, "Why haven't you been at church?" Of course, he loves President Trump because he talks just like Fred.

Another symptom of his age is that he loves the attention of young pretty women. He has always been a faithful husband but when young women come up to him he just perks right up and almost shows off. Well, this was the circumstance at a particular Sunday dinner with the family. He specifically was excited to talk to the two young lady Christian missionaries who sat at the table with us. He began to tell for the 100th time his experience of coming over on the boat from Germany to America. He then began to talk about how strong he was for his age. He described how every man at church his age is weak, fat, and out of shape. How if he got in a fight he could "kick their ass." He is a 5 foot 6 inch 140 pound skinny guy but thinks he has muscle.

Even though his legs looked more like pelican legs that day, he lifted up his pants to show the missionaries his "huge" calf muscles. As he slapped at them to impress, my kids were looking at their grandpa, laughing. He has always kept the dinner table entertaining.

He apparently thought that wasn't enough. He then said to the missionaries, "You should see my pecs. They are much bigger than my calves. Then to my mother-in law Ella's horror, he stood up and began to take off his shirt to show his chest. His pale white pasty belly and old chest was not a site that any young, unassuming, female missionary should ever have to see. At this point our family was laughing so hard we were in tears. Now topless, Fred grabbed his white undershirt and took it like a rope in a rodeo and began to swing it around and around over his head ready to swat it at the young ladies. They began to run and he took off after them. They were both being chased around the family room trying to dodge every swing of the shirt while Ella ran after him to stop the mayhem. Like I said, Fred could get away with anything.

Dinners like this have been a staple in our home. It provides a foundation to the day that speaks to family. It speaks to good times. It speaks to memories. It speaks to spending time together. It speaks to a consistent routine.

One of our favorite things about Sundays are our typical family dinners.

Recovery Day

The third and last routine I will describe may be one of the most important family lifestyle choices we have chosen to follow. It is a primary reason our family dynamic seems to have some balance to it. We have rarely been completely out of control with our schedules. Today I see many families barely hanging on. They have become slaves to their created schedules. Without a break, it just goes on day after day. There is no rest from it all. Yet it is something we each have the power to do something about in our own lives.

The routine that has made all the difference in the world to us is to take a break from our normal schedule one day a week. It is a recovery day. We happen to do it on Sunday, but for others it may fit better to be on a different day of the week. We call it a family day. From a religious point of view, we call it the Sabbath Day. The focus on this has paid huge dividends for us. It has become one of my favorite days of the week for many reasons.

Most religious people view the 10 commandments to be important. Keeping the Sabbath Day Holy is the 4th commandment. Most of the commandments have one verse to describe it. The Sabbath Day has four. It seems like God wanted to bring special attention to its importance. I think even though it has been discussed for thousands of years there has never been a more important time in history where this principle has had a greater impact.

Yet today, I view there are few people who put much focus on it. It seems to be no different from Saturday. There may be a few extra sporting events and possibly some church mixed in but for the most part it is a regular day.

Most churches create numerous services to accommodate everyone's busy Sunday schedule. In fact, there really isn't a day set aside for the Sabbath anymore. Now, it is a goal to simply fit in a church service somewhere on a busy weekend.

But sometimes simply fitting a religious event into our schedules can keep us from experiencing the full blessing available to us. Certainly, the time in church with our families helps us focus our minds above the normal hustle and bustle of life to worship our amazing God. This is the highlight of a day of rest. However, another blessing is simply resting the whole day from our normal routines of school, sports, work, house cleaning, bill paying, and the other elements of daily life. It's an awesome thing to focus on God, spend time with family, serve the community, play with the kids, and even take a nap. Just make it a different kind of day.

The Human Performance Institute has done research on seeking recovery. This company works with professional athletes to reach optimal performance within their discipline. The goal is to help their clients reach the ranking of #1 in the world. They have had success with over 16 athletes reaching #1.

The researchers studied athletes in their training regiments, across many different disciplines. They discovered that the training differs very little between the #1 athlete in the world and the 200th ranked athlete. These athletes are all very talented. They each have trained with great intensity for years, and continue to do so. They all have great coaches. What the researchers discovered as the only significant difference is that the #1 ranked athletes "seek recovery." They have created systems and routines to rest and renew themselves on a regular basis. They do something for recovery daily and they plan for periods of deeper recovery during the week. They also plan yearly times of R and R. They even seek recovery while competing.

As an example, when a top ranked tennis player finishes a point, he or she might transfer the racket from the serving arm hand to the other hand. This increases blood flow in the serving arm, allowing that arm and hand a few seconds of rest. Then the player might look at the tennis strings and stare, move his or her fingers around, as if adjusting the strings in deep thought. This relaxes the mind and gets the focus off the last point and onto the next. These mini breaks can take less than 15 seconds but can be a system of recovery throughout the match. It enhances the player's ability to compete at a high level of energy for hours.

In every sport, it is crucial to have recovery time for the mind and body. Any professional cyclist might be found on the couch for frequent rests throughout a training day. Runners have hard days and easy recovery days to keep from injury. This is not a new concept.

It is said that the body can only be at peak energy performance for 90-120 minutes a day. We each need multiple moments of recovery every day. I personally feel my stretching routine, which takes me 25 minutes a day is a must for my recovery. It is almost more for my mind than it is for my muscles. It allows me to have some deep breathing and clearing of thoughts that sets me up for a successful day.

My daily vision exercise is a recovery system. My daily prayers are a consistent recovery for my mind. Taking time to sit down and eat dinner with my family is a recovery system.

So, of course, a day of recovery will fulfill a similar purpose. God created us in every unique detail, so He understands our physical, spiritual, and mental need for renewal and recovery. This day of rest was made to benefit us.

The day my commitment to the Sabbath day began, was while I was attending the first annual business meeting of my career. I was 24 years old and right out of college. All the new financial reps went to Milwaukee, Wisconsin for 4 days of education and fun. We arrived on a Saturday night and checked into our rooms packed with four other guys.

The activities began on Sunday morning with a 5k race that had close to 10,000 employees competing against each other. This was my first month in the business and I had quite a chance to make an impression. I was probably in some of the best running shape of my life. I felt like I had a chance to either win the race or get onto the podium. I would be recognized in the general session. I would stick out. I would impress. This would be fun.

There was only one problem; I couldn't run. Since my mission experience, I had made a commitment that I would treat the Sabbath day differently and not compete on Sunday. That was a personal choice that was in line with what our church taught.

Everyone from my firm was in the race. As they woke up that morning and got ready for the race my mind was churning. I was dying inside. I wanted to run that race so badly. Thoughts went through my head, "Nobody here would think anything of it. I could do it just this once." "It's not like this is a sin." "Other people from my church are in it." I had all sorts of reasons to put on the running shorts and race to victory. This was just killing me inside.

Ultimately, I decided to stick to my principles and sit this one out. I sat in the room mad and frustrated. It bugged me that most races seemed to be on Sunday. But I was determined. I had stood for something when no one else was watching. In fact, it even made me look different and less cool to my work friends. They didn't understand. But there was some personal pride within me that I had somehow passed a test.

I then looked up the local church and went to services that day while the race went on without me. The winner was within reach of my capabilities but there was no David Shuley there to beat him.

From that day forward I consistently have lived by my own version of what that day should look like. I believe the whole day should be treated differently than all the other days of the week. It should be a rest from our "labors." Well, what does this mean? I view it far more broadly than just not working. It is that we should make it a different day completely that will give us time to rejuvenate. I don't believe God gives us any commandments to make us miserable or hold us back. These commandments should produce a better life. It should create closer relationships. It should bring us closer to Him. Everyone interprets this command differently. I don't believe there is one right way of resting. I am sure some could be critical of my attempt. But I will share what has worked for us.

We view Sunday as a family day. We have a few rules in place. These are the things we don't do. We don't let kids play with friends. We don't have them in sports where their games would be on Sunday. We don't go to athletic or entertaining events. We don't go out to dinner. We don't watch television, except for family movies. For a while we turned the phones off, but that got away from us. Now these are not absolutes. There are, of course, some exceptions. But this is our normal Sunday cadence.

Those are the things we don't do. That almost sounds like the oral law back in Jesus' day. But we found that in order to rest from the norm we had to cut these things out of our day. This was particularly hard as the kids became prominent in their sports. The norm today is to play on teams that compete in multiple tournaments throughout the year, with the final games most often being on Sundays. In fact, some of the regular season games are on Sundays. Families often spend Sundays scattered, going from one game to the other. Each one of our kids has been asked to be on these teams. We only let them, if the coach allowed them to skip Sunday games. We always looked at the regular season schedule to see how many games would be missed because of Sunday.

In professional sports, the pattern of playing games holds true as well. In almost every sport, the greatest finals are on Sunday. Whether it is the Super Bowl, the Masters final round, or the World Cup Final, the big finals are always on Sunday. This has been a big sacrifice for my family. I still read about everything with great interest. We do allow our kids to watch the Super Bowl as the one NFL game a year. But it is a sacrifice to limit everything else.

One thing that should be noted is that even though we have followed the no Sunday rule for athletics, our kid's abilities have been magnified. It has all worked out without Sunday play. One of our kids is a seven time cross-country and track high school state champion. Our three other kids made the high school soccer teams and have been captains for the school. I am not convinced we have to give up the day of rest to be good at sports.

If all we were to do is limit everything we did on Sunday, our kids would hate that day. Instead we have strived to make it one of our kids' favorite days. We want it to be good for them in different ways. We have eliminated most of the regular normal stuff so we have time to "do" many things. These are some of the things we do on Sunday: we go to church, have extended family over for dinner, go on evening family walks, play crazy basement family soccer, watch family home videos, take naps, visit the less fortunate, perform music together, have spontaneous dance parties, write letters to family, hang out, and just talk. Our longest conversations have typically taken place on Sundays.

I don't know if this sounds as fun as what a regular weekend day would be. It definitely is toned down. Sometimes my kids are even bored. But what we found is that it caused us to interact more, talk more, and goof off together more. We just end up being together more on Sunday.

I remember talking to my son Blake one evening in his senior year. I asked him what was his favorite day of the week? He said it was Sunday. It didn't surprise me, but it did make me smile. I knew he enjoyed being around family so much. He particularly liked church, his favorite pot roast meal, the family walks and of course family soccer.

The overarching benefit for us has been God time, family time, and giving our minds and bodies a rest. Because of this, I perform better at work, I perform better as a parent, I have more physical and mental energy for my week, and I have a balance to my life. This has been one of the most impactful routines in our family's life. I love Sundays!

A question to consider: What regular routines do I have that I am proud of?

CHAPTER 9

Forgiveness

"We cannot choose our external circumstances, but we can always choose how we respond to them." —Epictetus

It was a very normal morning at the office. While I was making some phone calls, my dad reached out to me and asked me to come down to his office. He wanted to talk about something. This wasn't too unusual. We often went to lunch and we spoke about work, family, and so forth.

When I arrived and sat down, he immediately started off the conversation with a bombshell. "David, I want you to know that I am leaving your mother. We are going to get a divorce."

My mind went into a fury. Where did this come from? How could this happen? How did I not have a clue about this? Even though my parents were separated for a while when I was young they had worked it out. Since then, they had stayed together for over 19 years. How could this be happening? If you had asked me that morning how my parent's marriage was going, I would have answered, "Great!" This was now the second time this has happened in my life and both times it came as a complete shock.

I asked my dad why? He stated he didn't love her anymore. I asked him if he had considered marriage counseling? He wasn't interested. I asked him if he would consider rethinking this for a while. He shook his head. I walked out of his office, devastated.

I didn't go back to work. My day was mentally over, so I headed home. When I arrived home and told Tonya the news, she hugged me, as I broke down and began to cry. I was just so sad. An overwhelming feeling of pain ran through me. So much of my life felt like it changed in one big painful piece of news.

The thought came to me, "Now every member of my family has been divorced but me." I knew how ugly it could be. I had seen the pain it caused. It is such a long process to work through.

I just didn't understand. Why? I called my mother to see what her perspective was. She was a wreck. She didn't want this. She felt abandoned and deeply hurt. She wanted to work it out.

Anger began to grow and grow inside of me. How could he do this to us? We had been a family. I felt we were close. Now what? This made me so mad. I was burning up inside. I needed to get out of the house and go run off some steam. So I put on my running shoes and got out of there.

After about a mile of running I came along a fenced off yard, where a dog came at me viciously with a loud bark. The fence luckily was a barrier between us. Usually, that would have given me a quick scare but on this day I wanted to kick the dog. I yelled at it, "Shut the hell up!" The run was not cooling me down.

The next day, after collecting my thoughts, I went over to my dad's office to talk to him. I, again, asked him why he wanted to leave my Mom. I just couldn't get why he didn't want to work on their marriage. He said, "I am not in love anymore and am moving on. He said something about how the events of 9/11 had convinced him to change his life. The thought of this just was so frustrating. I said, "That is bullshit," and just walked out the door, fuming.

If you know me, I have not said a single curse word on purpose since elementary school. It simply wasn't part of my personality. But in this moment it came very natural.

My dad moved out that day, and our family was forever different. I watched my mom go into a very deep depression. It was hard for me to see her struggle. Within 3 months she lost 60 pounds. She felt like she lost much of her identity. I did my best to see her often and comfort her as much as possible. I felt it my responsibility. Often I would get a call and need to immediately rush over for support. It was always such a downer experience. I would come home and feel like it didn't help her much. It angered me to be in that position.

The holidays came and went. We had young kids, which makes the season fun. But with my mother being so unhappy, there was a pervading gloom over everything. We bought her a dog so that she might have a companion. But it was a bust. She returned him within two days.

In the meantime my dad was doing quite well. He was already in a new relationship and really enjoying it. He wanted us to meet her and get to know her better. But even though she was very nice to us I found it very hard to accept her. I don't think he comprehended how much I was going through trying to keep one parent consoled then visiting him and trying to act as if everything was alright. Deep down I was hurt and it was hard to just push that aside.

One day my dad asked me how I felt about him. I didn't say much but I told him I forgave him. I meant it. Probably because I was taught at a young age to forgive because Jesus tells us to forgive. So that's what I did. I forgave him and my dad accepted it.

My dad still wanted to be a part of our lives. He called at least weekly to see how we were doing. I found that when he called I wasn't too excited to get the call. In fact, my eyes would roll. But I always answered it and then had a good and often fun time talking. This was interesting. Why would I not feel like picking up the phone but then enjoy talking to him? I soon came to realize that I really hadn't deep down inside forgiven him. I was still angry and hurt.

In the following year, my dad remarried and moved from Cincinnati to Newport Beach, California. He received a super job opportunity and ran with it. He continually called weekly to stay connected to me. This went on for 2 ½ years from the time of the divorce. The whole time I still wasn't excited to pick up the phone but enjoyed the conversation. I loved him but I think my view of him was defined by this divorce.

In the meantime, my mom still struggled. Her life gradually got better but at this time she still needed a lot of support. She had not completely moved on.

Then, one day an event happened that taught me about family, pain, and forgiveness. It changed everything for me. It was a gift.

Early in the morning, I received an urgent call from a friend. She asked if I could come quickly to her home. I was the Bishop of our Church of Jesus Christ congregation and had spent a lot of time with this family. She regularly looked to me for support.

That previous night her husband had tragically committed suicide. He shot himself in his truck in front of a group of people begging him to calm down. His kids were not aware of it and the mother wanted me to be there when she told them the news. Obviously I would not be going to work that day. I cancelled all my appointments and drove over.

This was terrible to watch. When she sat them down to talk, I knew what was coming. She then told them, and the kids burst out crying uncontrollably. Chaos erupted as the teenage kids ran out of the room screaming. I said nothing, knowing little of what to do. I sat there quietly until things calmed down.

After attempting to console the family for a while I took the 15 year old son out to breakfast. He was particularly close to his father. I probably wasn't too helpful but I was there. I felt being there was what was most important. I figured when people mourn I should mourn with them. True friends just show up.

The next couple of days I helped with the funeral arrangements. They asked me to conduct and speak at the service. I had spoken at funerals before but this one was a tough one. What do you say to family and friends when someone died in such a tragic way?

What I felt inspired to focus on was to have us not judge. We don't know the mental state of someone who commits suicide. We don't understand their pain. We are not in their shoes. We can continue to love them and cherish their memory and leave the judgment up to God.

I felt the service went well. I was satisfied with my message. Before we were to leave for the graveyard they gave the family a few minutes with the body before they would shut the casket permanently. I was there alone with the family.

As I watched them tenderly cry over the body one last time I felt so sorry for them. After standing there for a minute my mind began to drift into my own thoughts. For some reason I pictured my own father lying there dead in the casket. I pictured my time with him was over. No more phone calls, golf rounds, or laughs at dinner. He was just gone. A thought came to my mind, "Do I want to have the current feeling of anger and disappointments towards my dad for the rest of my life? Do I want this to go to his grave?" The answer was "No."

At that very moment I felt an immediate release. It was as if all the pain of the past 2 ½ years was just lifted off my shoulders. It was somehow just gone. All I could feel was the love for my dad. I pictured him lying there in the future at his passing with nothing but love for him. Tears came to my eyes and I began to cry. I couldn't stop. I just cried and cried. 2 ½ years of tears came flooding out. Others in the room assumed I was mourning over my friend's death but it was really a cry of joy. I had now truly forgiven my father. The pain was gone.

Tyler Perry once said, "The most important thing that I learned in growing up is that forgiveness is something that, when you do it, you free yourself to move on." This happened to me. The next time the phone rang and my wife told me it was my dad; I was excited to answer the phone. When I talked, I wanted it to be a long conversation. My feelings for my father were forever different. The divorce was behind us. When I looked at him, it wasn't through the lens of the divorce. I felt free in a way.

This was a gift from God. This was not my doing. I had not prayed to have the pain removed from me. I didn't come to this funeral with my father on my mind. I had pain and anger deep down inside that wouldn't go away, and God took the opportunity to bless me and teach me a lesson. He took this out of me. It was my final step to forgiving my father.

I had said that I had forgiven my dad for over two years but I truly hadn't. I thought I had, but I had not. What I learned through this experience is: just saying, "I forgive you" is not enough. We must check to see if we still hold a grudge. Because when we forgive we truly feel love for the person and stop dwelling on past actions. We no longer have anger towards them.

The principle of forgiving others is one of the major secrets to happy living. It is hard to be angry and happy at the same time. It is much easier to be happy without any anger. We have all met bitter people who for possibly good reasons have been consistently angry. They may have had unfair things happen to them. But their anger fills their persona. They are tough to hang around because they drain the room.

I have seen people offended by others who have held onto the grudge for years, carrying the anger with them everywhere they went. I have seen people stop going to church, stop going to family functions, and stop talking to their spouses. At the end of the day anger wears and wears on us, until we age physically, we are less fun socially, we are numb spiritually, and our relationships diminish. Holding anger is a weakness in our character. It is a sign of strength, not weakness, to forgive.

When someone has done wrong and brought pain into our lives, it seems that they would need to apologize and ask forgiveness before we would be called upon to forgive. And it certainly seems that the wrongdoer should have to change his or her ways before we would need to extend grace.

Further pain can be caused by people who are completely unrepentant and who never apologize. However, many times the offender could care less about the consequences of his actions. As much as we would like to see the person have true sorrow and repentance, the truth is: we need to choose to forgive for our own mental health and freedom from the anger and heaviness. I think it is important to understand this truth, so we can work on getting past this.

I have found that if we have the desire to forgive, most of the time we can do so and move on immediately. Sometimes it takes a little longer. And the most serious events of hurt, anger, and offense can take significant time. I find that for most really bad situations the five-year mark is a big one. I have observed this to be quite consistent. That was the case for my mother's forgiveness toward my dad. It took her five years for the anger to be gone.

I have tried most of my life to be quick to forgive. This has eliminated a lot of daily stress that could have existed in my life. But when I had a big event it took longer for me to get through the process. I always try to tell people: "If you find yourself not being able to forgive and still possessing anger, keep working on it. Be persistent. Pray for God to remove anger from your heart."

At the time of this writing it has been 15 years since the funeral. Since then, my father and I have had many great experiences together. We have traveled together, played golf together, mourned together, had weekly phone calls together, and have done many good things together. I would have had a very difficult time enjoying these experiences, if they would have even occurred at all, had I not forgiven him. In my forgiveness to him, I benefited the most.

A question to consider: Who do I need to forgive immediately?

Golf trip with my dad in Monterey California. Pictured at my favorite par 3 I have ever played. Shot a par on it too!

CHAPTER 10

We Are Going to Have Fun Together

"You're only given a little spark of madness. You mustn't lose it." —Robin Williams

Gordon B. Hinckley once said, "In all of living, have much fun and laughter. Life is to be enjoyed, not just endured." We have that quote on our kitchen counter at home as a constant reminder. We are not going to just endure life; we are going to have fun together. We do our best to do this. We haven't been perfect but it has been a focus. And to do it, yes, it takes focus.

There have been many times where the kids wanted to play soccer. As exhausted parents, we have times when we don't feel like doing anything but relaxing on the couch. However, I know it is my job to get up and take the time. I try to remind myself: PRIORITIES=TIME. So if fun is a priority I have to take the time with my family when I can get it.

My wife Tonya was particularly good at this. When our kids were all under the age of 11 we had woods behind our house. It was an adventure back there. One day, she took our kids to Lowe's and bought some wood, nails, and plywood scraps. With them she began constructing a fort in the woods. It was without much beauty but the kids sure loved hammering nails.

As the summer went on, the fort began to take shape. Most of the neighborhood kids began hanging out down there. I would come home from work to multiple hammers smacking at the nails. It was a miniature construction site. There Tonya sat with multiple kids from the street, acting like a general contractor.

Tonya was always in the mix building the fort back in the woods

Soon, the kids noticed beside the fort some trees that had thick vines hanging from the tops. They found that if they made a run at it, the vine would create a fun Tarzan-like swing. Our woods sloped so that when they would swing, the momentum created significant height before coming back to safety. They spent hours swinging back and forth to see what kind of height they could achieve.

Of course, Tonya was right in the center of the fun. She took her turn over and over swinging back and forth on the vines. It felt like an amusement park back there. Every kid in the neighborhood wanted to take their turn. This lasted for weeks. It never got old.

One day, while Tonya was taking her turn there came a crack and pop. The vine broke mid air and Tonya came down hard directly on her back. That really hurt. This was always a worry of mine with this adventure. Ironically, Tonya was the one who paid the price, not a neighborhood kid. She, of course, brushed it off. Luckily, the fall didn't break her back.

Many times I marveled at Tonya as I watched her play with our children. There were some great moms in the neighborhood but no one played with their kids and their friends like Tonya. Whether it was her drawing with chalk on the driveway, building forts in the woods, playing soccer in the basement, or sledding down the hills on a snowy night, she made it a focus to not just watch the kids have fun, but to be right in the middle of the fun.

Some of the best kind of fun is family fun. It doesn't have to be without other friends or extended family but it always seems to include family. We have a few principles to make sure life is fun in the Shuley home.

Choose To Play At Our House

We try to make our home the place that our kids want to bring their friends. We would rather have the neighborhood here than our kids hanging out elsewhere. We feel we can control more of what types of activities, movies, and trouble they might get into by having them under our roof.

To make it fun, sometimes our basement got destroyed and dented. The paint got scrapped and the noise level was deafening. We encouraged play versus just being on the phones or TV when friends came over. We created enough open space in our downstairs for small ball soccer to occur, gymnastics to take place, and forts to be built. We had a piano and microphone for music sessions. We had grass in the backyard to play football on. Our kids seldom went to their friends' house even as teenagers. The friends often came here.

We have a specific rule that is unique. We did not allow our kids to have sleepovers at their friends' home. We did allow our kids to have sleepovers at our house. This was a big one. It was for multiple reasons, the biggest was to protect our girls under my watch from anything inappropriate ever happening.

It was hard explaining to their friend's parents when their child had a birthday party and was finishing it with a sleepover, that we needed to pick up our child around 11pm. We never made an exception. We always blamed it on us being mean parents. But our kids knew better. After a while they never really complained. Besides, they had sleepovers at our house all the time and they knew how to make it fun.

This was all part of making our home the center of our kid's fun. We have rented a dunking machine in the summer, built a homemade ice-skating rink in the winter. We played ping-pong inside the house and played basketball outside. As our kids got older we built a swimming pool with rocks and waterfalls. All these things have been intentional to add fun to our lives and to have the center of it in our home. Besides the pool, these things didn't take much money at all. We can choose to have fun. It is a choice.

Winter ice-skating in our backyard with the neighbors.

We rented a dunking booth a few times for some summer fun.

Typical day in the basement. Blake pulls off his Michael Jordan dunk.

Basement soccer became a staple in the Shuley home.

The pool we built in our kids later years went to great use with their friends.

Choose to vacation

The baby blue summer sky cast light over the jagged "Valley of 10 Peaks." In every direction nature was on full display. Mountains were all around us. Evergreen trees surrounded the aqua blue lake nestled directly below the peaks. The smell of the needles in the clean wilderness air calmed my mind the minute we arrived. There wasn't much noise, just the occasional distant crack, pop, and rumble of glacier movements. Moraine Lake, Canada is simply one of the top five prettiest mountain scenes I have ever witnessed. We couldn't have picked a more perfect place or perfect day to go on an epic hike.

From our earliest days of marriage Tonya and I have enjoyed hiking together. We appreciate trekking through the wilderness and walking up to one of those memorable vistas. There is nothing like it. We can just sit and marvel at the enormous beauty of this world. So when we have picked vacation spots, they almost always included a hike with a view we had seen in a magazine.

Moraine Lake was not on the Canadian five-dollar bill for nothing. It had one of those vistas to remember. Today would be a family hike to remember. With our kids ranging from age 14 down to 7, we figured they could handle around a 7-mile hike. This would take us above tree line into grizzly country, which made us a little nervous. Bear signs were everywhere telling us we had to travel in groups.

At the beginning of the hike, we made our way up a steep section of the trail through the evergreens. Our oldest son Ethan was a high school runner and made it a workout. He ran up sections of the switchbacks. We made him stop and wait for us every 400 yards because of the risk of bears. He had the boundless energy of a teenager.

Once we made it above the tree line the mountains began to open up to us again. The backdrop was beautiful. We walked along the tundra with many beautiful mountain flowers sprinkled throughout the area. We kept walking uphill with our goal to make it to the top of the ridge so that we could overlook the valley on the other side.

Once we got within a half of a mile of the ridge we came upon some snowfields. This was mid summer but we were remote and high enough for snow to still exist. There were two snowfields that scared me a bit. Hikers had created a footpath along the snow. But if you lost your balance, you could fall and begin sliding to the bottom. There were no cliffs but it was steep. I walked nervously holding our youngest daughter's hand very tight. We made it across safely then up to the ridge.

What a beautiful view of both valleys. It felt like we could see forever. It was picture time and time to relax from the 3½ miles of uphill climbing. We passed out the treats and sat for a while taking it all in.

The Moraine Lake hike to the snowfields.

Going back down always seems easier. There was an extra spring in our step. When we came upon the snowfield again we noticed some college students had decided to slide down it feet first on their backs. It looked fun but seemed a little crazy. It did save 10 minutes of hiking which was nice.

My oldest son Ethan was right behind them and yelled to ask, "Can I do that dad?" I was uneasy but I told him, "Sure, just be careful." So he walked out to the middle of the snow path then in an instant, turned headfirst on his back and began sliding down blind. I yelled, "Ethan, what are you thinking?" He kept sliding and sliding headfirst looking up into the sky for over 200 yards. As the snow began to level out there was a massive rock pile. At first I was worried he might reach it without knowing it was even there. That could have been disastrous. But he stopped well before that. After the brief worry, we all cheered him on. He ended with his fists lifted in the air, screaming "Yah-Hoo!" I could tell he was proud of himself that he had done it. The college students that looked on were impressed. He had one upped them.

His younger brother Blake thought he had to do it now. He sheepishly walked out on the snow. He didn't go head first like his brother but he sat on his butt. He slid cautiously most of the way and at times got on his feet and ran down. We cheered him on the same.

Brooke was next. She always wanted to prove herself to her brothers. She had shorter shorts on, so when she got out there she had a different idea on how to get down. She thought she would go on her bum. But when it got cold she would stand up and jog down for a bit. This sounded good in concept. But when she slid about a third of the way down and stood up to begin jogging, the steepness of the hill plus her momentum made her jog turn into a run, then her run turned into a sprint; then she got going so fast her legs couldn't keep up. She began tumbling head over heels, completely out of control. It went on for what seemed an eternity. She finally got to the level ground and came to a stop. With snow crystals from head to toe and cold red cheeks shining in the sunlight she looked up with a smile and gave us the thumbs up.

We saw this unfold before our eyes as we were filming for a family movie. We could not stop laughing. It was a hilarious scene. We had witnessed this standing next to a Scandinavian young couple. They said our kids seemed so fun.

My turn was next. I went without incident. Then Tonya took Grace. They went down together rather carefully. Grace at seven years of age was not interested in having a Brooke moment. They would go slow and methodically. Grace slid the whole way on her bum. It was safe but it did freeze her backside to the point that it made her cry. When they reached the bottom we tried to calm Grace down by trying to warm up her frozen butt cheeks. Tonya basically put her hands up her shorts and held onto her cheeks for about five minutes as Grace whimpered on and on. After the warm hands did the trick, Grace began to settle down. The resume of a mother is large. We can now add "Butt Warmer" to the list! I laughed really hard as I sat and watched this. I imagined other hikers wondering what the heck Tonya was doing with her hands on Grace's backside. During this funny scene Tonya said, "No pictures." Too bad, that would have been a good one for the photo album!

As I look back on this adventurous hike I can't imagine having more fun with my family. That day we had a blast together. We spent six hours with no cell phones, no outside influences, and no distractions; just nature, conversation, exercise, and fun. I have noticed that our kids rarely have longer sustained conversations than on a hike. It is quality time together. In life, creating these magical memories is the icing on the cake. It is what we live for.

As a family we have learned to love vacations. As we have gotten older some trips have become more expensive but while our family was young they didn't cost much at all. One thing is for sure, trips don't always go as planned. A particular trip to Arizona can serve as an example.

We were excited to be on our way to the airport. It was a well-anticipated family trip to Arizona to spend some time with relatives. Also the warm weather sounded like a dream. We had bought some inexpensive tickets out of Indianapolis, which was 110 miles away. It was worth the drive, especially when you have six tickets to buy.

We had rushed out of the house after I had packed all the luggage in the back of the car. We finally arrived at the airport after a long drive. It would be nice to just get on the plane.

As I began to unpack the car, each child grabbed their bags. I closed up the car and began to walk toward the terminal. Then Tonya said, "Where is my bag?" I turned to her with great alarm, "You don't have your bag?" She said, "No, where is it?" I went back to the car and looked. It was nowhere to be found. I had left it in our master bedroom closet at home. Now I was in deep trouble. She had asked me to bring it out to the car and I had forgotten it.

What do I say? What can I do? We are over 100 miles from our house and our flight leaves in less than 2 hours. We were going for a weeklong vacation and my wife had nothing. No clothes, underwear, make up, bathing suit, not a thing. She had nothing.

Needless to say Tonya was not happy with me. I was in the doghouse with no way to get out. At this point there wasn't much I could do or say. We left the parking lot and sheepishly I walked into the terminal to check in our bags.

Trips don't always go exactly as planned. But even that trip provided a lot of fun and good memories. When we arrived in Arizona Tonya went through all her sisters' clothes that could possibly fit her. She then went to the store to buy a couple things. It wasn't perfect but Tonya moved on from it after the first day. We ended up having a super fun time in the sun. Unfortunately, Tonya has a good story in her back pocket that she can always use against me for the future.

I feel there are many reasons to go on trips. For me, it starts with providing something to look forward to in our busy work/family life. Sometimes when I am melancholy, I focus on the next trip that has been planned. This directs my mind from something negative to something positive. It is like a good shot of dopamine. I always want something in my life to look forward to. If I can't think of one, I create it.

Vacations supply some of our family's best moments. An unknown author has said, "Take vacations, go to as many places as you can, you can always make money, you can't always make memories." I believe memories are based on moments. We tend to forget the mundane elements of the trip and focus on and a few great highlights. Those highlights are what we share with others. I have noticed that most of the great memories of life are specific moments where we were touched by a beautiful scene, a connection with others, a spiritual high, an achievement accomplished. Many of these moments can be found in our choice to leave the daily grind and take a break to see the world.

Choose To Create Traditions

We enjoy the annual traditions we have created. We specifically have done this with the set holidays, which make it easy for fun. Whether it is coming downstairs to Easter baskets, running in the firecracker 5k on July 4th and enjoying family fireworks that night, dressing up for our famous Shuley Halloween Party then finishing the night with a scare in our haunted house, eating a delicious Thanksgiving feast with extended family, celebrating birthdays not just on the day but all weekend long, or observing the month-long Christmas traditions that include decorating the house, enjoying zoo lights, making gingerbread houses, caroling to the people experiencing hardship, visiting manger scenes, enjoying Christmas morning with cinnamon rolls, and dinner with the kid's talent show at night. These things have become traditions that have woven lasting memories into our home.

Our annual Shuley Halloween Party is always a hit.
Guardian of the Galaxy year we never looked cooler.

One of these traditions noted occurs every year the Sunday before Christmas. There are few things that bring more Christmas cheer than this tradition. It is just plain fun. Last year was a good example of it.

We found five families in the area who had little money for Christmas. Two of the families we knew from church; the others were inner city families that a friend arranged for us to help. We called them in advance to see the specific needs of the families. Then we arranged for some friends to help with the gifts. These friends came with their families to our house at the appointed night to deliver gifts. We arranged in advance for those receiving gifts to be there when we arrived. Everyone met at our house before for some Christmas cheer before heading out.

It all started out as usual with a lot of goodies, gift organizing, and prepping the convoy of the areas to which we would be driving. Then we split people up and headed to the cars. Everyone left through the front door to get in their cars, waiting for us to be the lead car.

When I opened the door to the garage to get to my car, I found a raccoon standing right in front of me. It immediately hissed at me as it stood its ground. I was startled, having never seen one in such close quarters before. I quickly grabbed a broom to poke at it to get it to run away. It only hissed louder, not budging an inch. In the meantime, everyone was waiting in the cars wondering what was taking me so long.

Tonya came up to the door and said, "A raccoon? What the heck. Hold on, I will be right back." She turned and darted off. At this point my brother and kids were marveling over this courageous raccoon. Within seconds, Tonya came back to the door with a pistol in her hand. She aimed at the raccoon and started firing. The little varmint took off running toward the corner of the garage. We all stared at Tonya in amazement. That was the toughest thing I had ever seen her do. No fear. Luckily it was just a BB gun, so it wasn't a blood bath out there. But still, Tonya scared us a bit. My brother's eyes were wide open and said, "I have learned to never mess with Tonya."

Unfortunately, the raccoon was still in the garage hiding behind some garbage bags full of Goodwill clothes. Because everyone was waiting, we decided to just leave the garage door open in hopes that the raccoon would sneak out after we left. He had to be scared to death, not to mention full of BB's.

This was not the normal start to our Christmas festivities. But we carried on. The convoy headed out and soon arrived at our first home. We all got out to sing carols to the family. They were so happy because they said they had never had carolers come to their inner city home before. The young daughter in the family opened up her unicorn stuffed animal and broke out into a huge smile. Her mother said it was her favorite. We sang another song then headed to the next destination.

When we arrived at the second stop it felt more like Halloween than Christmas. It was a dark, dilapidated, dirty two-story home that had a chain link fence surrounding it with only mud and dirt for a front yard. All the lights were off and it looked like the only thing inhabiting it were ghosts.

We asked ourselves, "Is this the right house?" This was the correct address but the house looked abandoned.

We had arranged with each family in advance the time we would arrive, so we expected them to be here. But it didn't look as if they were home.

The house looked so cold, dark, and scary that no one of the group wanted to go in through the chain link fence to knock on the door. It was too intimidating.

After a little discussion, I convinced one of the teenage boys in our group to go knock on the door to see if someone was home. He cautiously opened the fence and made it a couple steps toward the house when all of a sudden an enormous muscle ripped dog came roaring out the front door. Our young friend ran for his life as the canine charged at him with a ferocious bark. He barely got through the gate and shut it behind him as the dog rammed his head into the fence. Then the dog ran back and forth along the fence line, leaping a few times to try to get over the fence to reach our crowd. He finally gave up and calmed down. All of us stood with our hair on end. We couldn't believe what just happened. Then we broke out laughing at what had unfolded before us.

Then, a small, dirty 14-year-old boy emerged from the front door, with his young sister in tow. He looked like a poor child right out of a Charles Dickens story. We asked the boy if his father was there. He said, "No." That irritated me because I had talked to the father and he had told us he would be there. I got the sense his dad was possibly a drug addict and had left these kids many times alone in this condition.

At that point I didn't know if the 20 of us were supposed to carol to these young kids or not. But then someone broke out with "Santa Claus is Coming to Town." The kids stood there awkwardly listening. As we were singing, their teenage sister came walking up the sidewalk. She seemed fairly mature, and we were able to discuss with her the particulars regarding the gifts. After unloading them to the smiles of the needy children, we piled into the cars for the next delivery.

Immediately, all the teenagers in my car talked with enthusiasm, laughter, and mixed emotions about what had just happened. The house, the dog, the kids, the presents: this was a mix of "The Amityville Horror" and "The Christmas Carol" all wrapped together as one. Our hearts went out to the children in that house, but we were glad we had been able to hopefully add some Christmas cheer to their lives.

When we finished all of our deliveries we said goodbye to our friends and returned to our home. To my frustration, the raccoon was still nestled in the garbage bags in the corner of the garage. He was probably so traumatized from earlier that he didn't want to move. So after much hissing and growling I figured a way to poke him from a different side angle, which made him make a run for the exit. The drama was finally over and no person or animal was killed in the process.

What a fun night of mixing service with fellowship! Few things can create better lasting memories than a meaningful and fun family tradition.

Frank Sonnenberg wrote on the topic. He said, "Traditions help form the structure and foundation of our families and our society." He lists seven reasons why traditions are so important:

1. Tradition contributes a sense of comfort and belonging. It brings families together and enables people to reconnect with friends.

2. Tradition reinforces values such as freedom, faith, integrity, a good education, personal responsibility, a strong work ethic, and the value of being selfless.

3. Tradition provides a forum to showcase role models and celebrate the things that really matter in life.

4. Tradition offers a chance to say "thank you" for the contribution that someone has made.

5. Tradition enables us to showcase the principles of our Founding Fathers, celebrate diversity, and unite as a country.

6. Tradition serves as an avenue for creating lasting memories for our families and friends.

7. Tradition offers an excellent context for meaningful pause and reflection.

Our family traditions have created a structure to our year. Family thrives on structure. There are many things, especially around the holidays, that we do every year. Our family expects and looks forward to these events, which produce many of our most fun memories.

A question to consider: In what ways have I chosen to have fun in my life?

CHAPTER 11

A Balanced Life

"Balance is the perfect state of still water. Let that be our model. It remains quiet within and is not disturbed on the surface." –Confucius

My first luxury sports car was a 2002 silver BMW 330S. It had all the bells and whistles a young executive could ever ask for. I was in my mid 30's and I thought I was so cool. It drove from 0 to 60 faster than I had ever experienced. The rear wheel drive felt very different but seemed to encourage speed. As I drove through tight turns it handled like a fast go-cart. This was truly an adult toy.

After two weeks of enjoying the car, I found myself at work on a cold winter day. During the afternoon we got clobbered with almost a foot of snow. I made a mistake not leaving work early to beat the snow and traffic. In the Midwest it doesn't take much for the streets to become a mess, and city services often do not have enough snowplows to handle a bigger event.

What normally takes 15 minutes to get home took over an hour, as the freeways were at a standstill. Snow was piled all over the streets. I noticed many times that the rear wheel drive on my car caused me to fishtail. The sports tires basically had minimal tread. It felt like driving in an ice skating rink with snow piled on top. I was worried I would put my first dent in my car only two weeks in.

Luckily, I made it all the way to the bottom of my street with no incident. But I worried because my road was quite steep and then I would have to turn left into my even steeper driveway to get up into my garage.

Initially, I felt pretty good as I was driving up the snowy street, but when I reached our house, my tires began spinning without moving forward. I felt like a drag racer at the beginning of a race, revving my engine and spinning my tires, except that I was not moving. So I put my foot on the brake and just sat there parallel to the street. I looked up at my house on the left, wondering how I could possibly turn and go up my driveway.

My wife saw me on the street and came out on our covered front porch to watch this predicament. I decided after some thought that I would just turn left and try to somehow park on the street in front of my house. I concluded it would be impossible to get up my even steeper driveway with no momentum.

I turned my wheel and the car moved in the direction of my house. But as it went perpendicular to the street, the lack of tread of the tires allowed the car to begin sliding sideways down the hill. I quickly opened the door and stuck my leg out to try to stop the car's slide. This was, of course, a useless effort, and the car continued to gain more speed. I was completely out of control. Tonya told me later that my eyes had a terrified look, like I was on the Titanic as it was about to sink into the abyss.

In a few seconds I was able to straighten out the car to head straight down the street. My next problem was that there was a UPS deliveryman who had parked his truck in the middle of the street to make a delivery. There was no way for my car to stop. I was headed for a collision right into the back of his truck.

I began honking my horn as loud as I could. Luckily the man was in the back of his truck organizing his packages and not at the front door of the neighbor's house. He noticed me coming in for a direct hit, so he hurried out of the back and ran to the cab. He started the truck up and began to drive off within seconds of direct impact from my BMW.

He kept his distance from me, and as the street began to level off I was able to come to a stop. I sat in awe at what had just transpired. I was so lucky that my little sports car had no damage. I had learned my lesson. I parked the car at the bottom of the street and walked home.

I think of this event because it illustrates to me how sometimes in life we can get out of control. We can feel like we are about to crash if we don't slow down. I can't think of any better way to describe the teenage years of raising kids. The schedule and pressure put on the family seems to be at its peak during those years. If we don't create habits to stay on top of it, we can be overwhelmed and feel like we have literally zero balance in life. I have some suggestions that have helped me.

One is to be sure I keep each of my main priorities in mind. A balanced life seems especially difficult when we are focused exclusively on only one part of life. I have seen colleagues lose their marriages over having a singular focus on their careers. I have seen families lose peace and balance over their kid's athletics schedules. I have seen this lack of balance in academia, too. There are examples everywhere. Of course, there may be times in life where a balance in life isn't possible. Going through med school might be a good example. However, the problem with having only a singular focus is that other areas of one's life will usually suffer. If left unchecked long term, this can lead to burnout and lack of true joy in life.

A balanced life can mean different things to different people. My own view of balance is to have time for health, family, spirituality, and work. There may be other elements very important, but for me, these are what matter most. These areas combined bring me the greatest joy and satisfaction in life. It is a feeling of long lasting fulfillment. Therefore, I plan my week with the focus to spend time in all of these areas. Over the years, it has become my natural cadence and is now just the normal way of life.

Health

I want to discuss health first because of all four areas this may be the largest factor of a fulfilling life. I will illustrate with an experience I had a few years ago.

I had just paid $1,000 dollars to attend a 2-day seminar with some out of town high achievers at my company. The speakers were to share insights and methods on how they had become successful. I was excited because we would be learning from the best.

The event started at 8am. That morning, walking downtown, I felt a little twinge in my stomach that didn't feel quite normal. I brushed it off because it didn't come on too strong. But by the time the meeting began, I had started to feel nauseated like I was coming down with the flu. I said to myself, "This can't happen today. I have paid way too much money to just go home because I don't feel well."

I sat there taking notes but my stomach got worse and worse. I started to feel a bead of sweat develop on my forehead. My stomach continued to turn over and over. I looked at my watch and we were only an hour into the seminar. I felt horrible.

Eventually I couldn't take it anymore. I stood up to walk to the bathroom. As I began walking, my stomach was screaming and I felt I might throw up. As I approached the lobby bathroom I felt it coming on. I dashed through the door and opened the only stall. As I went for the toilet to begin to heave, I passed out.

I awoke to footsteps and the voices of my coworkers coming into the restroom during the break from the meeting. At first I was confused as to why I was lying on my back between the toilet and the wall of the bathroom stall. I then realized I had passed out. I had no idea how long I had been laying there.

When I sat up, I noticed thick puke splattered all over the wall. I must have passed out in the midst of letting it all go. I had definitely missed the toilet.

I had a major headache but I thought I'd better start cleaning up my mess. After wiping things down, I walked out into the bathroom. Other people were still in there using the urinal and washing their hands. I tried to not be noticed, but a few people saw me and said "David you don't look so good." I looked at myself in the mirror and saw that my face was ghostly white.

Still determined to tough it out, I went downstairs to lay down to see if I could feel better soon so that I could stay and learn something from the seminar. It is amazing how $1,000 can affect decisions.

After around 45 minutes of lying on a couch I started feeling stable. I said to myself, "I've got this." So I picked up my note pad and headed back up to the meeting.

I began to get interested in the topic they were discussing, until about 30 minutes had gone by. Then, I started feeling my stomach turn again. I was thinking to myself, "Are you serious?" After a few minutes it started to build and build until I said to myself I may have to throw up again.

This time the nausea came on fairly quickly and urgently. I got up and began to head out of the room but realized I might not have time to get to the restroom. There was an adjacent kitchen area in the back of the room where a coworker was preparing the lunches for everyone. There was an open entry into the kitchen area with a wall barrier so food could be prepared in a somewhat sanitary environment.

I ran past the food and coworker to get to the sink. I then started to throw up into the sink so violently that my knees buckled. I almost fainted for a second time. I heaved multiple times making quite the background noise for the meeting.

When things settled down, my coworker who was preparing food looked at me and said, "Dave, you should go home." I conceded, she was right.

As I look back on this, I realize that no matter how hard we try, no matter how badly we want something, no matter how important, it is almost impossible to do anything at all when we are majorly sick. That day, I could not even sit in a meeting. That is why I feel health may be the most important element to focus on for a happy and well-balanced life. Without health it is hard to spend quality time on family, work, or church. It is hard to do much of anything. If we each think back to the last time we were sick, we remember how little we were able to actually accomplish. I have always heard, "If you haven't solved a person's physical hunger you can't solve his spiritual hunger." The physical is paramount in so much of this life.

In my wealth management practice, I frequently do financial planning for people who have all the money they will ever need for a happy retirement, but their current lifestyle is so bad, they might not get to truly enjoy their retirement years. Their mobility and activity level is already so limited that they may spend too many days of their "golden years" in a doctor's office.

I often think that I should focus my clients more on their health than their investments. It will mean far more later. But few focus on their health as much as they do on their money.

I once heard a doctor say, "Twenty percent of people are born with great longevity genes and will have few health problems, regardless of how they take care of themselves. Think of George Burns at 100 years old smoking like a chimney. Twenty percent of people are born with bad genes and will not be healthy even if they take great care of themselves." He then said, "sixty percent of people are born with average genes and how each one takes care of himself directly relates to his capacities and longevity." So, if we practice a healthy lifestyle day to day, there is an 80% chance that our lives will be long and vibrant. I like those odds. It makes it worthwhile for me to focus on my health.

There are many different formulas to living a healthy life, and I don't want to imply a certain way is the best. One-way does not fit all. However, there are a few principles that seem to stick out as important.

I have heard from multiple doctors that the single greatest thing we can do for our health is to elevate our heart rate above 135 beats per minute for 30 minutes a day. That is it. Whether we run, bike, swim, walk, lift weights, or yoga, it is important for our system to elevate the heart rate.

I use another reference point for this principle. I just want to make sure I break a sweat every day. I typically can't do that without elevating my heart rate in some way.

For me, working out is typically one of the highlights of my day. To some, exercising might feel like work and be something they dread. However, I have found that most people who exercised regularly before graduating from high school are far more likely to enjoy physical exertion as an adult. As long as they exercised consistently for a reasonable period of time and enjoyed it at some level, this seems to help them enjoy the discipline later in life. In my case running in high school is associated with a lot of great memories and is still enjoyable today.

As a parent, I have focused on helping my kids discover something they enjoy doing that can easily be continued in adulthood. I look for something for each of them that go beyond the sport they happen to play. As an example, a high school football player will most likely not be playing much football as a 50 year old. But he may enjoy lifting weights during the season, which could be a discipline that will carry over to adulthood, and influence his health enormously. Whatever the exercise, I feel it is very important to start young because of the likelihood that exercise will be viewed as fun versus a chore in the future.

Eating Habits

Healthy habits involve more than just exercise. What we put into our bodies is the fuel that keeps our engines running. I remember a particular weekend with my middle school son. On Friday he had his friends over for a sleepover. Tonya was nice to him that night and provided pizza, Oreo cookies, candy, and some popcorn. They played and ate, watched movies and ate, played soccer, then ate some more. It was a fun night for everyone.

The next day, our son said goodbye to his friends and then went to a school function where at the end they served treats for everyone. The kids loved it. That night we had grandpa come in from out of town, so we went out to dinner and had barbecue ribs with dessert for everyone. It was paid for by grandpa, so no one held back.

The next day we went to church. Our son's Sunday school teacher was everyone's favorite because she provided candy and cupcakes for all the kids. They listened while they ate.

That evening we had our normal Sunday dinner, and with my dad in town, we, of course, had a feast, complete with his favorite, a bowl of ice cream.

This is the life of children today. This is just normal life. It is no wonder we have an obesity problem in America. Our kids are bombarded with unhealthy food everywhere they go. It has become part of our culture to have most events revolve around treats. We have seemingly constant access to processed food, which is, sadly, far cheaper than healthy food. To serve a family a salad with grilled chicken on top is far more expensive than buying a premade macaroni and cheese dish. It is not surprising that America is one of the only places in the world where poor people are overweight.

Good health is about 80% of what we eat and 20% is our active lifestyle. Eating good food really matters. Having said that, there is nothing better to me than rhubarb custard pie on my birthday, pumpkin pie on Thanksgiving, or a Reese's blizzard from DQ on a date with Tonya. So to enjoy life, I think a healthy balance needs to be met.

Ideal for me is 80% percent of the time to eat good food and stay away from desserts. 20% of the time I will, as my kids say it, "Go Ham" on certain days. Holidays are always full of food and dessert. I allow myself to let go. It can be fun. But when I am training for a race I may stay away from desserts for a couple of months at a time. That has been the balance for me that has allowed me to stay within a 20 pound range for the past 30 years.

We have tried to teach our children good eating habits. I know we have not been perfect parents in this area. It is hard to strike a balance of focusing on good health and also not making it too big of a focus. Today, children can develop eating disorders from pressure from others, especially parents. What we say in this area is very important. Words are powerful.

My goal with my girls is to always discuss health and not size or looks. My girls will always be beautiful to me, regardless of size or shape. I do my best to tell them this regularly. Psychologists have stated that it is best to compliment your children about their looks but not every day. It is better to compliment them each day for a variety of reasons, so they will realize that character, and behavior are more important than looks. Examples may be comments like: "I noticed how thoughtful you are with your younger sister today." or "I admire how you focus on your school work and earn great grades." "You had such a good soccer game today, I love your hustle."

I try to keep the ratio around 1 out of every 5 compliments about their looks. "Grace, you sure played beautifully at your concert tonight." "I love your hair today. It is so pretty." "I like that dress on you." Through these compliments I hope my kids feel confident in themselves about how they look but even more important, I hope they see the quality of their character is of even greater value.

Mental Health

I had decided for Grace's birth that I was going to take a full week off from work to help out. For the birth of our previous three kids, I had taken only a couple of days off, assuming Tonya's mom and mine were enough. But looking back, I realized they didn't stay more than a couple of days and Tonya really did a lot on her own. This time I wanted to be here for her. It was the right thing to do.

About 4 days after our daughter's birth, I was alone with Grace, rocking her to sleep when the phone rang. I hesitated to pick it up because I didn't want to wake her. For some reason, I decided to answer it.

After I said, "Hello" I heard on the other end of the line a soft voice say, "David, I have taken a lot of pills. I am going to die. You need to take care of my son." As I stood there bouncing my baby to keep her asleep, I was in shock at what I just heard. Had this friend really just overdosed? Where was she located? Was she by herself? Was there something I could do? What should I do? I paced back and forth and sent a silent prayer up to God to help me help her.

This was an old family friend who had experienced a lot of tragedy in her life. She was abused as a child, widowed early in life, had no money, job, or education. Her experiences influenced her to feel mental pain every day of her life. The only support she had was her friends and her church. But every step of her way was a major uphill battle.

When one of her sons, as a young adult, died of a drug overdose, it was the final straw. Her depression ran deep. She couldn't take it any longer. She had decided to take her life. She just wanted the pain to stop.

I asked her, "Where are you?" She would not tell me. She didn't want me to come get her. She only told me that she was in her car somewhere. She then said to me, "David, I want you to take care of Matt when I am gone. I need you to do this for me." I thought to myself, this is not good. He was only around 7 years old at the time. We knew him well and would have been there for him, but at this moment I told her, "No." I said, "You have to take care of your son. Matt needs you and no one can take your place." She said, "No David, I just can't do this." I said, "Yes you can." We went back and forth and she didn't budge at all.

I tried to explain to her that she could get better. That she wouldn't feel this way forever. I tried to instill some hope. It was useless. She just kept asking if I would take Matt. I kept telling her I would not. I kept asking her where she was located. She would not tell me.

At this point we had been on the phone for around 30 to 40 minutes. The whole time I paced back and forth holding my newborn in my arms, just trying to somehow save my friend's life. On the phone as her words started to sound drowsy and slurred, the hair began to stand on the back of my neck. I could sense the drugs had begun to take effect. I knew there was very little time left before she would doze off to her death.

I began to plead with her to tell me where she was located. She resisted. I asked her again and again. She continued to resist. At this point she could hardly respond.

Then, for some reason, she blurted out that she was at a rest stop on Interstate 75 just south of Florence. I couldn't believe she finally told me. I think the drugs must have affected her ability to think straight and she didn't realize what she had just done. I knew exactly where she was located.

I told her we would send help and immediately I hung up. I called her oldest son and told him to call the ambulance and get there fast. He lived in the area. The rescue squad arrived and raced her to the hospital. They were able to pump her stomach in time to save her life.

When I got off the phone, I was overwhelmed. I said to myself, "What just happened?" It was almost a surreal experience. I was shaking inside and on the edge of tears as I looked down at my beautiful baby girl peacefully sleeping in my arms. I had never been through anything like this before. I had no training. I didn't know what to say. All I know is that she finally gave in and told me where she was located. I was so relieved and thankful for God's help.

What is weird is how things sometimes work out. This occurred before I had my own cell phone. She called our home telephone number. I was never at home on a Thursday during midday where I would have been able to answer it. I was at the right place at the right time. Had I not decided to stay home for my wife I would have never been there to save my friend.

The best part of this story is to see my friend 15 years later. At this point through much counseling, support from others and God's help and direction she is living a happy life. She has raised her family, become self reliant, retired from her career, and is serving others. She is no longer clinically depressed and lives in peace.

She serves as a great example to me of faith, endurance, grit, love, and the knowledge that people can heal. I remember going to lunch with her years before this episode when she told me, "David, there isn't a day that goes by where I don't feel pain from my past and the present. It is constant in my life. Pain and depression are always by my side.

I felt inspired to tell her that day that there would be a day when this pain would be gone. God could take it from her. He would show her the way. At that time, she had looked at me as if I were crazy and just didn't understand.

She was correct. I didn't understand. But I have a belief that whatever situation we find ourselves in, there is a way for peace. God has a way and He has a hopeful future for everyone.

Today there is a mental health crisis in America. More than half the prison inmates have mental health issues. I think people run through life with a pace unheard of in the past. If we don't work on maintaining healthy beliefs, right attitudes, and responsible actions, we can easily find ourselves overwhelmed by the consequences of our own poor choices or the sometimes-harsh circumstances of life around us.

My advice in this area is two-fold. First, everyone needs someone to talk to for counsel and guidance. Whether we have in our past abuse, trauma, self esteem issues, anxiety or situational depression, we should talk to someone. Wise counselors say that burying pain deep inside does not take away the heartache; the trauma will simply rise to live an uglier life later… and it may come boiling out when we least expect it, perhaps when we are having a mere disagreement with our spouse, who was not involved in any way with the pain of the past. But the buried pain comes bursting out anyway, adding trauma and pain to an innocent conversation.

Some feel there is a stigma to seeing a counselor or getting help. I don't. I have personally counseled with the bishop at my church for situations I have had. I have talked with my doctor about situational anxiety in the past. I have had family members use therapists to overcome certain issues. I have prayed to God for direction and advice with problems. All these are counselors in my mind.

The important point here is: we can get through things if we use all the resources around us and if we deal with the actual issues. Waiting until later in life simply makes issues more complicated. It truly is possible to overcome whatever holds us back! There is always hope! Joyce Vissell once said, "An unresolved issue will be like a cancer with the potential to spread into other areas of your relationship, eroding the joy, lightness, love, and beauty."

What I saw with my friend is it takes some courage and patience to get through things. Most of the time we might initially take a few steps back to move forward. But eventually we can find a way. Shannon Adler has said, "Courage doesn't happen when you have all the answers. It happens when you are ready to face the questions you have been avoiding your whole life."

I realize that anything I have ever achieved at a high level, whether in sports, business, mental health, finance or hobbies, has always seemed to happen with the help of a coach/counselor. I believe that we usually can't achieve at the highest level we are capable of, on our own. We need to learn from others with more experience. I currently have a running coach, a business coach, and a spiritual mentor. I even hired a financial planner for my wife and me, even though I own and lead a financial planning firm. I know I can still learn from other perspectives.

It's not true that only the weak ask for help. In fact, the opposite is true: it is the strong and successful that seeks good counsel and advice. That has always been the case with successful people.

Another observation with mental health involves two practical ways to improve.

First, studies have indicated that 15 minutes of exercise could be equivalent to 1 Zoloft pill. That seems to be a much-improved way of receiving relief. Exercise releases chemicals in our bodies that cannot be replicated in a laboratory. Daily exercise is great for mental health.

Second, having a meaningful purpose is important for mental health. Early in my career, I had a business coach answer a question that really stuck out to me. Having just hired my first employee for my company, I asked, "What do I do to keep my new secretary happy?" He responded, "Don't worry about making her happy, if she is challenged in a positive way, she will be happy." That made a lot of sense. When we are working hard toward something that is meaningful to us, we feel a sense of productivity and usefulness that does something for the soul. Most of the time the journey is the real excitement, not the award at the end.

I once had a mentor suggest that almost any problem with his children could be solved with work. He said that teaching children to put solid effort into a job can do wonders for their attitude and self esteem.

I have also observed just the opposite—where laziness and too much time on our hands can lead to depression. Sitting around, day after day, is not good for the soul in so many ways.

That is why I suggest that having a purpose and challenging us toward excellence, is a practical way to maintain strong mental health. If we have nothing in our lives that is doing this for us, we should dream of something. Everyone probably has a number of goals that would put a smile on their face, if achieved. Michael Jordan often quoted his father as saying: "It's never too late to do anything you wanted to do." It's a well beloved adage that we never know what you can accomplish until we try.

I recognize that some mental health issues are beyond our scope to improve on our own. For some, medication is required to help with chemical imbalances that exist. As mentioned earlier in the book, my friend would have greatly benefited from certain medications. That is why professionals can often make a huge difference. I do believe we need to first do all we can do without medications to see if naturally we can overcome our difficulties. But if that isn't successful there should not be any stigma attached to using medication.

Focus On Family

The summer after I graduated from high school I worked up in Idaho on farms, roguing potatoes. It was a mindless job that didn't pay a lot of money but did give me a super dark tan from the waist up. The $3.35 an hour only while working on the field did not yield much college money by the end of the summer. This, to the disappointment of my parents.

One weekend in the late summer I had a chance to visit friends in Utah for the weekend. There were four of us going down which would make it a cheap trip.

After a fun short trip we were driving back to Idaho in the late evening. It was a 3½-hour drive, and we had reached the halfway point, near the outskirts of Malad, Idaho. We were driving in a small Mazda hatchback that was barely large enough to fit the four of us with our belongings. I had fallen asleep in the back seat of the passenger side. I had removed my seat belt for maximum comfort. The only person who was awake was the driver. She was drinking caffeinated drinks and listening to music to keep her awake.

At one point, she decided to change the song on the boom box that was set between the two front seats. As she did, the car began to drift to the left. When she looked up, she was startled to see the car heading for a reflective barrier. She sharply corrected the car to the right, but had overreacted and we were now headed off the road the other way. At 65 miles per hour, the car began its skid.

I woke to squealing tires and an out of control car. We sped off the road down into a depression between the road and a hill. Immediately, the front of the car caught the embankment and began to flip. I have never forgotten the sound of squealing tires and then the ferocious pounding of the car as it tumbled out of control. It is a horribly loud sound. There is nothing any of us could do at that moment. There was no holding on, there was no controlling ourselves, we were at the whim of whatever the car wanted to do. We tumbled over and over, pounding and smashing as we somersaulted along the side of the road. We rolled 2½ times before abruptly coming to a stop upside down.

The accident destroyed the car. It lay there upside down like a dead animal on the side of the road. All the windows were blown out. The roof was smashed down to the level of the dashboard. There was a smell of oil in the air. The engine had stopped but the lights were still on. Steam rose from the engine like a smoldering fire.

I was knocked out briefly, but soon woke up to find that two of my friends had already climbed out of the car. The girl who was driving the car was still in the car with me. She was screaming hysterically because of mistakenly feeling blood all over her body. She kept saying, I feel blood, I feel blood all over me." She later found it was a massive amount of oil that had splattered all over her from the wreck. At that point I frantically told her we had to get out of the car.

As we crawled on the broken glass through the window opening to get out of the car, we were finally able to get to our feet. To calm her down, I walked up to her and hugged her. As I held her I could feel her shiver in fear and shock from what just occurred.

After she began to calm down, we walked up onto the road to flag someone down for help. The dark night sky in this rural area made it difficult for anyone to see us. The car was upside down below the road, so the lights could not be seen by those passing by.

This was not a busy section of the interstate. A car would drive by every couple of minutes but it was so dark they wouldn't even see us and kept driving. As I continued to wave at the cars I began to feel woozy. I must have sustained a concussion, because I felt like I would faint if I stood any longer. So I lay down on the road as she continued to jump up and down waving and screaming.

Finally someone stopped. It must have been quite the scene with my body lying on the road next to a frantic girl begging for help. Then, to see the mangled car upside down off the highway and two other young men wandering around the wreck. This was not a normal stop in the middle of the night.

Our new friends called 911 and soon the ambulance came to help. I was still lying there when they arrived. They kept me on my back while they packed me into the ambulance. They were worried about my head, so they kept me stabilized.

After we arrived at the hospital, the doctors checked us out. It was amazing; I only had minor cuts and bruises. One friend broke his thumb. Another had some lingering neck issues. But we were all safe and without serious injuries. Each of us felt really sore for the next couple days as if we had been beaten up in a fight. But all of this was minor.

We knew it was a miracle that we didn't all die. None of us had buckled our seat belts. None of us were thrown from the car. The car didn't drive off of a cliff or crash into a tree. As I look back, I feel so blessed.

This event had a big impact on me. I realized just how quickly our lives could be seriously altered or ended. Just like that, we can be gone. Just like that, everything can change. I became more intentional about making the most of my time, realizing that if I didn't take advantage of the now, I might not get another chance.

As I grew older and got married, then had a family, this principle became even more relevant to me. I saw how limited and precious time with Tonya and each of our children truly was. I realized that if I didn't take advantage of the time I had with them, I would regret it. Even without a premature death, our kids are out of the home before we are prepared for it as parents.

I remember when our kids were young, we sometimes felt so overwhelmed and so tired that we wondered when our child-rearing responsibilities would ease up. Then, all of a sudden, we had a child who reached high school and the next four years flew by so fast that we found ourselves at an emotional graduation ceremony.

To have a balanced life, experts advise that whatever family situation we are in, it's wise to focus on family time. Over and over again, we learn that Time=Priorities. So if we want family to be a focus of our balanced life we will want to carve out time throughout the week to restore ourselves and each other as a family.

If we want to assess our own priorities in this area, we might ask ourselves some of the following questions:

- Where do you have the most fun? Is your family involved?

- Who do you serve the most? Is it family?

- When scheduling conflicts come up, is family put first?

- Are career goals larger than family goals?

- Are your spiritual connections closest within your family?

Mental health counselors say that emotionally fulfilling lives are those in which family relationships are strong, dependable and nurturing. It is the healthiest way to live. I have never met anyone who regrets focusing on their family. It is a journey worth the effort.

One observation I would make regarding focusing on family is that it is messy. If there is one thing I learned from serving as a bishop and counselor of a congregation for six years is that EVERY FAMILY HAS DYSFUNCTION.

I remember going to church and looking at certain families that seemed to be so buttoned up. They never seemed to argue or fight. They just seemed to always show love to each other. Today we see the facade every day on Facebook or Instagram posts. Everyone seems to be doing so well except us.

My experience is: dysfunction at some level is completely normal. It happens in every family. If we could see the problems others have in their family, we most often would not trade them for ours.

Jeff Foxworthy once said, "If you ever start feeling like you have the goofiest, craziest, most dysfunctional family in the world, all you have to do is go to a state fair. Because five minutes at the fair, you'll be going, you know, we're all right. We are dang near royalty."

I guess we just need to be thankful for what we have. When we feel this way it influences us to focus more and more time on them. Over time we find that there is nothing greater and more important. We will not waste the time that we have been given. We will live today for our family and not wait to spend time together in the future when it might be more convenient.

Spirituality

I became a bit nervous when a fellow cyclist suggested he wished he could have brought a third lung to the race. As I stood at the starting line with my bike, I didn't have a clue what a bike race to the top of one of Colorado's "Fourteeners" would feel like. I was told that mountain climbers start to use oxygen around 14,000 feet. Now I was going to attempt going as fast as I could on a bike to the top. My training on the hills of Kentucky at 300-800 feet above sea level was not exactly ideal for this race.

The Mount Evans Hill Climb is an annual event that attracts a large number of cyclists who want to test themselves to see if they can race to the top of the highest road in America. It starts in Idaho Springs at 7,000 feet and finishes 27 miles later as the road ends atop Mt. Evans at 14,130 of elevation. The grade is pretty steady and steep most of the way. At the age of 40, I was in some of the best shape of my life but had no idea how I would react to the altitude.

As the race began I had high hopes of winning the race. It consisted only of men in my age group. I was used to competing against 25 year olds, which made this race feel somewhat more to my advantage.

We started off at a 1% to 2% grade for the first six miles. No one took off fast because we knew the road would tip up at six miles and there the race would truly begin. In this early section of the race, we were in a peloton, riding around 18 miles per hour, which felt completely comfortable. After about 3 miles I happened to look at my watch to see what my heart rate looked like. Typically cruising at this effort it would be around 135 bpm. I was surprised to see my monitor show 170 bpm. That is where the rate should be at the end of a race going all out in full sprint mode. Only occasionally did my heart rate ever reach 180.

I thought my monitor had to be messed up because there was no way it could be accurate, based on how slow we were riding. It irritated me, because I felt like it could be helpful to see accurate data later in the race. So I kept riding along and ignored what I just saw.

After a few more miles, the pace began to pick up a bit and the hill was starting to tip up some. My legs were as fresh as could be but I noticed cardiovascularly I was feeling a little messed up. I looked down at my monitor and saw 170 bpm still. I began to wonder if in some way it was accurate.

Then as I looked up, I began to see stars. My eyes seemed blurry and I started to realize I was breathing deeply on each breath. My heart rate really had been 170 this whole time. The altitude had completely taken over and we were not above 8,000 feet yet. I realized at this moment that I needed to let the leaders roll ahead and slow down a bit. Maybe I could reconnect later.

When we finally hit the mountain and it pitched up to 10%, within a half a mile I knew I would not win this race. My legs were fine. But I had no engine to propel it forward. Where was my third lung when I needed it?

At this point, riders were passing me occasionally, one after another. There was nothing I could do about it. I had nothing to respond with. I just kept my pace the best I could. I did this for about 40 minutes and finally settled down into an effort that I could handle. But others were still passing me and I didn't pass anyone.

Eventually, another person passed me and I said to myself, "That is enough." So I sped up and got in his back wheel. No one else was going to pass me. "I can do this," I thought.

Well, that lasted about 100 yards. The increased exertion burned me up quickly and I had to drop off his wheel. I was just completely exhausted. I didn't have it in me to stay with him.

At that moment, I went around a corner and had reached the tree line. There, the conditions are too harsh for the trees to grow, and all the riders can see is tundra, a few shrubs, and exposed rocks. As I went around the turn with no trees to protect us, an enormous gust of mountain wind hit me directly in the face. It almost slowed my bike to a stop.

I felt this was the final straw. I had been obliterated by the elevation, I had zero energy, I had wind blowing me backwards, and I still had 10 miles and 3,000 feet to climb to go. The mountain had no mercy.

I decided at that point that I didn't care what speed I went, what place I took, or what my overall time was, my goal was to make it to the top without getting off my bike. Just keep pedaling and reach the peak.

With that new goal in mind, I climbed and climbed; at times I was only going 4 miles an hour. But I didn't care. I just wanted to reach the top.

An ultra marathoner, David Goggins, has said in his podcasts that when you are completely spent in a race and tell yourself you can't go any further that you have only spent 40%. You actually have 60% left within you that you haven't discovered yet. He said to keep going, keep moving forward, you can do more.

I have always felt that this is true. It requires the athlete to believe he can do this. It requires belief in that remaining 60%. With that belief, the mind pushes the body into new levels it has never discovered before. Belief is power. Belief is what can move us to greatness.

When I reached 13,000 feet, my belief was put to its greatest test. I was only a couple of miles from the finish. I was going up a steep section of switchbacks. As I looked down the clear mountain valleys I could see for 100's of miles. I passed mountain goats grazing in between the rocks. There were no cars, no people, no noise, no wind, and no air; just the bike and me.

I hurt badly. I had been riding for 2 ½ hours with a 170 bpm heart rate. My kidneys were aching, my legs were burning, my mind was fuzzy, my vision was slightly blurred, and I had a sensation that I had never felt before nor since. I COULD HEAR MY HEART BEATING. It was so quiet as I rode up only four or five miles per hour. My heart was thumping so hard that I heard each beat. It was almost like I was listening through a stethoscope placed on my chest. It was something so odd. That can't be healthy?

After one of the most difficult athletic events of my life, I finally reached the summit. I crawled off my bike and sat on the side of the parking lot looking into oblivion. I had done it. I had made it! I believed I could make it and I did. I had used the belief in my mind to override my body when it told me to stop over and over again.

I had reached 12,000 feet on the way to the top of the
Mount Evans Hill Climb Race.

The only thing that got me to the finish line that day was my personal belief that I could do it. I believed I could endure the pain until it was over. I believed that if others could do it, I could do it. I just believed, and my body followed.

Belief creates power in our lives. Whether that is belief in ourselves or belief in a higher power, it moves us forward to greatness. I feel most people fail to understand this adequately.

My belief and faith in myself has a foundation in my belief in God. I believe that I am a son of God; literally one of his offspring. I have his DNA at my very core. I believe God did not create us merely to be His worshippers. He created us to be His heirs. Because that is true, I can accomplish grand things. He sure does. So if I am His offspring I should be able as well. I can think much bigger. Like the Apostle Paul said, "I can do all things through Christ who strengthens me." (Philippians 4:13) I believe this scripture is meant as inspiration for all Christ followers.

The focus of following God and believing His word are important elements of a balanced life. It is a blessing to incorporate spiritual disciplines into our daily schedules just like we are blessed by daily exercise, daily work habits, and daily time with family.

When I think of keeping my spirituality strong, I think of a fire. In my teenage years I spent a lot of time hanging out by a campfire late into the night. I was involved in scouting where we went on numerous camp-outs in the mountains of Utah. Sitting by the fire is one of my favorite times in that scene.

One thing I noticed is that, as a quality fire burns hot, the logs turn a bright crimson red color. If I were to grab a set of tongs, pick up one of the logs and toss it out of the pit, it would quickly begin to cool. Soon it would turn a gray ash color and fizzle out. Yet had I left it in the fire with the other logs it would still be burning strong.

I think our spirituality is similar to a fire because we are stronger together. It is certainly possible to be spiritually strong on our own, but growing our faith alongside others can be an accelerant. I believe our faith can be especially strong, if it starts and has its foundation in the family. If our family can have spiritual experiences together, we are closer to each other and my individual connection to God is also multiplied.

The focus of my week includes a few things to instill spirituality into our family life. Every family is different and one should adapt to its individual needs. There is no one right way. But I will share what has worked best for us.

First, we pray together. This includes all meals we have as a family but also before the kids leave for school, we have a family prayer. The old saying, "A family that prays together stays together" has some merit.

Second, we reserve 15 to 60 minutes on Monday nights to have a

"Family Night." What we do for Family Night can differ each week. Some weeks it is simply a prayer, a short spiritual thought from the scriptures, a quick game of indoor soccer in the basement and a treat. That pattern probably represents 75% of all Family Nights. Some weeks, instead, we might deliver cookies to a friend. Some weeks all we did was play a game. But each week we were together and it had a spiritual tone to it.

There definitely have been weeks where one or more children were not in the mood for Family Night. A few times, my kids said 'this is boring'. In fact, a few nights were such a failure that I am just glad there were no cameras filming our "loving" family. But the weekly cadence throughout my kids' childhoods made this a great way to start off our week.

As I mentioned earlier, a third way we have incorporated spirituality into our family life is taking Sunday off from our normal routine to "Keep the Sabbath Day Holy." I discussed it thoroughly earlier so I will not elaborate. But going to church was definitely a central element to the day. Our church also supplied a Wednesday night youth activity for our children during the week in which we actively participated, as well.

With the consistent elements of prayer, Family Night, Sabbath Day, and church involvement, we have woven spirituality into week, and it has become a foundation to our family.

I share the spiritual disciplines our family has enjoyed, realizing that in today's society the importance of organized religion seems to be fading. At the time of this writing, research published from journal PLOS ONE showed that 4 out of 10 Millennials say they are religiously unaffiliated. The journal stated, "For the new study, the researchers reviewed four surveys conducted between 1966 to 2014 involving 11.2 million American adolescents between the ages of 13 to 18 and compared it to their research of Millennials. They found that Millennials were less likely to attend services, less likely to say religion was important in their lives, and less approving of religious organizations than Boomers and Gen X'ers were at the same age. Millennials were also less likely to describe themselves as spiritual, suggesting that religion has not been replaced by spirituality."

So, some Millennials might occasionally wonder: what is the purpose of organized religion? Why do we need it? If they felt their faith and church had a positive impact on their lives they might consider it. But it seems like that isn't where they feel most people will find the impact and answers to life. My church has done this for me. Without it, much of my personal and family way of life would be very different. Much of what is good in my life I attribute to my beliefs and to growth through church.

There are a few principles that I feel one should consider for church to be most impactful in life.

First, I believe it should be a home-centered, family supporting church. Not the other way around. We are there to have the church support our family in our spiritual goals, not to have us go to support the church.

This means our most spiritual lessons can be taught in the home, not the sermon from church. A good church would facilitate this by creating materials for us to teach in our home and creating wholesome activities for our families to enjoy together.

When the corona virus pandemic invaded the world and churches were closed and we spent most of our time together in our homes, we were able to put into practice our home-centered elements of our faith. With the lessons and videos produced by our church, along with the scriptures, we were able to have very spiritual moments together as a family and our church experience didn't miss a beat.

A wisely run church would also offer opportunities to serve others, create moments to be reverent, and offer opportunities to make commitments to God. The best churches offer times of fun and experiences of connection to others as we worship together. Church should be a place of love not fear.

Belonging to a church that is home-centered and family supporting is a great way for our spirituality to be a red-hot log in a much larger warm fire.

Second, I believe that the church needs to stand for God and His teachings, and we need to have a personal testimony of it. It is important to have conviction in what is taught and to be able to verbalize it.

If we follow God's teachings and belong to a home-centered church, these beliefs will create a foundation on which our family can operate, and will form a solid basis on which our decisions can be made. This is important, because there will be times in every person's life when beliefs and convictions will be tested. So it is extremely helpful if the beliefs of the church match what we believe deep down inside, so we can receive assurance in times of challenge or doubt.

I will give you an example of faith principles that have instructed my life. These are my beliefs and may be very different from the faith of others. The purpose of sharing them is to suggest topics for thought, prayer, and perhaps discussion with others.

1. I know that Jesus Christ paid for my sins, died, and was resurrected.

2. I believe God is very aware of us and directs our lives.

3. I believe we can communicate with our Heavenly Father through prayer. I receive answers in many ways, including impressions from the Holy Ghost and scripture.

4. I feel a love and support through the Holy Ghost

5. I believe God wants us to live joyfully and peacefully; therefore if I follow his commandments, they lead me to a happier life.

6. I believe wickedness never was happiness.

7. I believe prophets of old, as well as those today, can lead us closer to God through revelation.

8. I believe our bodies are temples from God that house

our spirits and should be treated with great care.

9. I believe honesty is of greatest importance.

10. I believe true religion is visiting the lonely and feeding the poor.

11. I believe love increases most in our lives through service.

12. I believe families are eternal in nature.

13. I believe one of the first questions Christ will ask me on the other side is, "How did you tend to your wife's needs?"

14. I believe my greatest joys are found in my faith and family.

15. I believe it is essential that we make commitments to God through baptism and other ordinances.

16. I believe we are literal children of God and that he wants us to become like him and live with him for eternity.

17. I believe when we finally learn all of God's grandeur that we will feel so humbled by our nothingness.

18. I believe that I can accomplish anything that is His will.

19. I believe the same sociality that exists with us on earth will exist in heaven.

20. I believe it is only upon the merits of Christ that we can be saved.

21. I believe in studying scripture. Every question I have in life can be answered through it. It is also a major way God speaks back to me.

This is what I believe. I attend a church that is aligned with these convictions. My children have been taught those principles at church and are surrounded by others who share the same basic beliefs.

When people bring up deep questions of faith, I usually point them toward scripture and recommend taking time to pray and ponder what they learn so they are not tossed to and fro by every new idea. Then they should ensure that the church they attend is aligned to those same ideas and principles. It can make the church experience much more impactful for them and their family.

Third, I want to share what cannot be left out of today's church experience. It is the multiple structured ways within the church to personally serve. In our church, one service opportunity is that we are assigned a few families to watch over to make sure their needs are met and to ensure they feel loved.

One of my assigned families is a single father who had been very ill. He'd had an operation during which his intestines were accidentally punctured, and much of his body was poisoned from the bile. This traumatic event shocked his body and put him into a coma for three months. Even after he came out of the coma, his entire body was still weakened from the bile, especially his intestines and stomach wall.

When my teenage son and I first visited him, he had been home from the hospital a couple of months. He couldn't move much at all. He had an open wound in his stomach area, because his intestines were so affected by his bile. He would die if the skin were closed up. He needed almost a year before his blood would not be too toxic and another surgery could be performed to fix the intestines and stomach wall.

When he first explained his problems to me, he lifted up his shirt and grabbed his intestine from his side and pulled some of it out. It was a reddish color and balloon-like in elasticity. He exposed about 6-10 inches of it. He squeezed and inflated it like a half blown up balloon. It was one of the grossest things I had ever seen. I had never viewed someone's organs exposed that were not in the midst of surgery.

Temporarily, this was his new life, and he was depressed knowing that he still had another nine months before his next surgery. His life was on a couch with a lot of pain.

He got around in a wheelchair because the poison also affected the bones in his legs. His house was not equipped for this at all. For example, his front door had a couple of steps leading up to it. He had to get out of his chair with the help of others to get through the door. Assisted, it still took 15 to 20 minutes to get from his couch to his car.

I felt this was unacceptable. I had to do something about this. It was my responsibility to do so. He needed a ramp built to allow him to wheel himself directly from the car into the house. I knew through our youth group at church we had the manpower to get this done quickly.

I called the leader of the youth, and within two weeks we were there on a Wednesday night, digging postholes and nailing the boards together. It took us two separate group visits for the 20-foot ramp to be completed.

I was so glad to see my two boys and 10 others spend their time helping out someone in need. The boys found it fun to build the structure but more importantly I think they felt the great spirit of compassion and satisfaction that comes with hard work for others. To this day, they bring up memories from that service project.

My kids along with other youth from the church built a ramp for a friend in need.

The service project wasn't all work and no play. The youth are always fun.

It's wonderful when the church offers a reservoir of opportunities to serve, especially for the youth of the church. True religion is found in serving God and the people of this world. If church is just something we show up for to hear a sermon, then walk away; it will be hard to sustain spiritual growth. I believe it is one of the major reasons we see many faiths struggle to keep the rising generation involved after they leave home. They have not had service to others ingrained in their souls yet. Making a difference to others is the heart of any good faith. Without it, the religious experience can be hollow.

I have seen our kids serve in many ways through our church. Whether it is helping with the actual service, giving a talk in church, helping me visit our assigned families, or going on a two year full-time mission somewhere in the world, these experiences have created a tradition of service within our family that is our standard. (At the time of this writing, I went to Texas for mission work, my wife went to Utah, my oldest son went to Ukraine, and our second son is currently in Brazil. All at a young age, serving people of those respective areas for two years. Hopefully our two girls will take opportunities to serve after they graduate from high school.)

If I didn't belong to an organized religion, much of this would not have happened. I am so thankful for my faith. I hope others find that appreciation as well.

Work and Career

When we have health, family and spirituality in our lives, we are well equipped to be effective at work. Mike Ertz once said, "The number one driver of exceptional performance is self confidence." A balanced life is an accelerant to self-confidence.

Making the best use of our time and talents at work is a part of maintaining a balanced life. Whether our career is in the workplace or in the home managing the household, we all have valuable work to do. Our chosen profession requires our attention throughout the week. It consumes, and often requires, a disproportionate amount of our time. God gave us work to add dignity and purpose to our lives. Meaningful work is good for our souls. Work often provides the solution to many of our problems, both financial and personal. It is also a key element in how we view ourselves. In a man's case, I have not seen anything wreck self-esteem as much as unemployment.

Since self-confidence is a main driver to success at work, it is important to figure out how to continually increase your confidence. Mike Ertz continues, "Recognizing and replicating success is what drives self confidence."

Brooke, our daughter, can help illustrate this principle well. When she was a sophomore in high school, she and two of her friends decided to submit a video to a talent show contest. This was not just the local high school talent show. It was at a Mega church, which had a stage and sound system to rival any concert venue.

Brooke had taken guitar lessons for a couple of years and was just learning to pick, but had never really performed in front of anyone. Her friends' only performances were in the high school choir.

They videoed themselves with all three girls harmonizing together while Brooke played the guitar. They then submitted it to the contest. Apparently they were one of 104 entries, and only five of the entries would be invited to perform in front of 1,500 people for a live show.

Miraculously, Brooke and her friends were picked to perform. It was funny because they had submitted this on a whim, and now they were put in a situation that was way out of their league and out of their comfort zone. They would be competing against some young bands that had performed for years. They were even asked to submit their groups name and they had never thought about it. They came up with the name, "Galilee."

As the day of the show approached, they practiced daily to get their performance ready. They were not focused much on stage presence; they just wanted to get the song right.

The day arrived and we went to the church. People were everywhere. It felt like a normal concert with a large audience, large TV screens everywhere, props, cameramen and the works. There was a buzz in the air.

All the performers were corralled backstage in a holding lounge. When it was time for them to perform, the cameraman interviewed the girls and broadcast it to the entire audience. It wasn't rehearsed and the girls stood there like deer in the headlights staring into the camera. Luckily Brooke spoke up and discussed what the "band" was about.

They then walked out on stage. As they began to perform, they had a lot of nervousness in their voices. They were a bit overwhelmed by the grand stage that they were on. Brooke was able to play the guitar without a mistake, but the singing and harmonizing between the girls had been done far better in rehearsals.

As a father, I was still so proud of my daughter. Galilee had gone from nothing to this overnight. They did their best and received a lot of good feedback from the night. They were probably the 4th best out of five acts, but it was a huge win for them.

This experience became a springboard for them. All the bands were asked to perform at a small local concert venue one month later. Each band was to have a five song set to fill the night. As a band they only had one song. This was a major challenge to decide on what five songs to sing and to then have them concert ready.

Even though they were all busy high schoolers, they practiced daily to get this right. It was amazing to see them learn from the first experience. They realized they had not had any stage presence and had not been confident when they sang, but they had felt good about the song and knew that they harmonized well. They wanted to replicate what was good and practice to get better with everything else.

When the next concert came, they were ready. We were so proud as they stood on that stage in a much smaller venue with a smaller audience and played a five song set that was far superior to all the others who played that night. They were incredible, confident, and entertaining for the crowd. The challenge was no longer too big for them. They had confidence built off of the first performance.

They later went on to win multiple high school talent shows and they even sang the National Anthem at the FC Cincinnati professional soccer game in front of 22,000 people. They did it without feeling overwhelmed. They were in their space.

Brooke and her friends singing the National Anthem
at the FC Cincinnati soccer game.

I find this example is so much like our careers. We need to put ourselves in situations that challenge and stretch us, perhaps even intimidate us. Then, we need to learn from those experiences, and apply our newfound wisdom and skills over and over again until they feel natural. An anonymous author said, "Challenge yourself with something you know you could never do, and what you'll find is that you can overcome anything." That is the way we grow and become successful in our careers.

I find it amazing that most people do not put themselves out there enough. Some of my most memorable appointments at work took place when I was a young salesman meeting with a CEO or a professional athlete who was way out of my league. There was very little I could help them with at the time, but I tried my hardest to convince them to work with me. I failed almost 100% of the time. That is alright. Over time with a few successes I got more and more confident and today I have many very successful CEOs as clients. They are really good clients and relating to them feels quite normal to me now. If I had never allowed myself to be uncomfortable I would have not likely have reached the heights that I am at today. So whatever our career choice may be, if we attempt tasks that seem above our abilities, it will serve to our advantage, long term.

It Never Hurts to Ask

The other tip I would have for work life is a quote that I have used with my kids a thousand times, "It never hurts to ask."

When my son Ethan was a sophomore, he was a really good runner for his age. In fact, he was the best distance runner for the high school. Like all the runners, he was interested in the Eastern Relays, which was one of the most prestigious track meets in the country. The best runners from over 15 Midwest States showed up to compete. On Friday night under the lights, the meet featured three heats of the two-mile, and one of them was for only the elite runners. The organizers of the Easter Relays separated these heats to create really fast times for college recruiting.

The cut off for getting into the elite field was a 9:45 for the two-mile.

30 people had qualified. Ethan had only raced twice that spring in the two mile and had a best time of 9:48. We thought it would be beneficial if he could get into the elite race, instead of trying to win the second best heat. He thought he could go for a PR in a faster race.

I talked to his coach about it and said, "It never hurts to ask, can you just try to convince the officials to let him in?" His coach was more than happy to try. With only minutes before the race he came back with a big smile and told us they made an exception and let him in. He did some great coaching that day.

Ethan smiled, but was a little nervous. He would be the lowest ranked seeded runner in the heat. There was a runner in the field he had heard about who was a sophomore as well. He was the top ranked sophomore in the country. Ethan told me that his strategy was going to stay right on that guy's butt the whole time until he couldn't do it anymore.

Well the gun went off and they started out at a blistering pace. The first lap was a 67 second lap. Then the second one was the same. Each lap Ethan would stay right behind the sophomore, even going out to the 4th lane at times to get around other runners. He did everything he could do to not lose contact.

Each lap they were consistently hitting 67 or 68 seconds on the splits. At the mile mark he came through in 4:32, which was only a few seconds off his mile PR.

The pack began to thin some on the 5th lap. Ethan was still right on his target and I was in the stands freaking out that he was still hanging on. The 6th lap went by and he was still there. I was just screaming, "Hold on, hold on!" I was in utter shock that he just clocked another 67 second lap.

Then with a lap and a half to go, the leaders began to make their moves. This included the sophomore Ethan was tracking. There were only about eight of them left in the lead group at this point. Ethan could not keep up with the new surge but he didn't bonk. He held on and held on until he finished the last lap and finished the race in 6th place with a time of 9:13. The winner was the nationally ranked sophomore with a time of 9:05. Ethan beat his PR by 35 seconds. His time was ranked 4th in the nation at that point in the season for sophomores. He has run many exciting races including seven Kentucky State Championships but this is my favorite race of all his high school events. He did something remarkable and something I wouldn't have thought possible at the time. After the race, his smile was so large because his time surprised him most of all. Sometimes we have no clue what we are capable of.

Ethan's finish in the Eastern Relays as a high school sophomore.

All of this would never have happened if we had been too timid to ask for an exception. Ethan would have run in a much slower, easier race and probably won it. But the experience wouldn't have been close to what ended up happening. The motto, "It never hurts to ask" is really true.

I find that in my career and in everyday life, this motto is often the key to getting a lot done and being far more successful. Sometimes as a business owner, I delegate tasks to my team that I know that I could do myself. This challenges them to stretch their skill levels, while allowing me to focus on my relationships with my clients, which is my genius. Sometimes I have to ask people to do something they don't feel like doing, but they agree, for the overall good of the group. Sometimes an employee must gather the courage to ask for a raise because he or she deserves it. Implementing the motto, "It never hurts to ask," is often the only way to accomplish important things.

I believe that many times people are simply not ready to offer something, do something, or initiate something without being asked. They need that nudge, that desire, to help someone before they will act. Sometimes people would have never considered it in their minds. But when asked, they think about it and often come to the conclusion that the request was a worthy idea.

Most of the time, the worst thing that can happen is that someone will say 'no' and we are in the same spot you were before we asked. I am sure there are occasions when it would have been better not to ask, but my experience suggests that asking rarely creates a problem. However, I don't make a habit of asking over and over after being told "No." I don't think any of us want to become an irritant to our employers or coworkers.

So work and career are very important components to a balanced life. Additionally, they are an important part of our self-esteem. We may spend more hours at them than any other area of our lives. Since they are such a big facet of our lives, we want to develop excellence in our skills, just as we want to strive to be at high levels with our health, family, and spirituality.

Questions to consider: Do I feel balanced in my life? What of the four elements: health, family, spirituality, or work do I need to focus on now?

CHAPTER 12

Halftime

"The real test of a man is not when he plays the role that he wants for himself, but when he plays the role destiny has for him." —Vaclav Havel"

It was Marguerite's first time on an airplane. It was Nick's first time west of the Mississippi. It was Alan's first time to southern Utah's national parks. These friends of my kids were headed for an adventure. As I sat on the airplane with my son Blake, my daughter Brooke, and three of their friends, I said to myself, "This ought to be fun."

They were headed to a BYU soccer camp in Utah because they all played on the high school soccer team and wanted some instruction and great play with others. One cannot have too much soccer. I had decided to take them a few days prior to the start of their camp, so I could show them some of the beauty of the West. Our first stop was Canyonlands National Park.

The drive through the state was not a long one. We were rocking to "Malibu" by Miley Cyrus, joking around, having a good time. It seemed like the 3-hour drive took 30 minutes.

When we arrived at Canyonlands the evening sky was burning. We sat on the edge of a cliff overlooking miles of red and orange natural carved rock with the Colorado River winding through it all. The kids' eyes were wide open. They had never seen anything like this. We could see for 50 miles. Nothing but beautiful desert rock stretched out before us in every direction.

Marguerite was so excited to be there she told Brooke, "We have to carve our name in the rock to remember this forever." I quickly told her that this is pristine nature and we should probably keep it that way. Plus, the National Park probably would chase her out of here for it. She had never even thought of that. We all laughed and chuckled.

As the sun began to go down, the colors began to peak. I told the kids, "It is hard to believe this morning we were in the Midwest and now we are looking at this. We are not in Kentucky anymore." They were less chatty at this point as the splendor before them took over. It was almost a reverent moment as the sun crept over the horizon. The sky was now bright orange and red like the rocks below. This scene was unlike anything they had ever seen before. It was a perfect moment. I will never forget it.

On this trip we would go on three hikes in Arches and Canyonlands National Parks, hike the top of Snowbird ski resort at 11,000 feet above sea level, hike to Stewart Falls on the back of the Great Mount Timpanogos, and they would compete at the high level BYU soccer camp. It was such a new experience for each of them that it was fun to watch.

On the drive back to the airport, I said to myself, "It can't get any better than this! I love being with my kids and their friends." Those are some of the best kinds of trips. There is something about being around young people. Maybe it's the mentoring element. Maybe it's how active and adventurous they can be. Maybe it is the difference that I feel I can make. But whatever it is, I love it.

At sunset the first night of our trip in Canyonlands National Park.

In his book, "Halftime," Bob Buford compares life to a football game. It has a first half and a second half of play. For the first half he said, "You probably rushed through college, fell in love, married, embarked on a career, climbed upward, and acquired a few things to help make the journey comfortable."

"You played a hard-fought first half. You may have even been winning. But sooner or later you began to wonder if this really was as good as it gets. Somehow, keeping score did not offer the thrill it once did."

For me, typically, the second half of a football game is the most exciting part of the game. It is where the game really gets intense and usually it is where the game is won. However, most people look at themselves half way through their lives and wonder what do I want to do with the second half? It's almost as if they believe the exciting seasons of life are all behind them. They look back for happy and meaningful times versus look to the future.

Bob Buford points out that the second half cannot only be meaningful but can be a RENAISSANCE. The best part of it is that we get to choose how our life adventure plays out. He believes that what we need to do is clarify where we want to focus our energies for the second half. Our focus needs to be narrower during this second half of life and centered on something that challenges us and something we love. He suggests we have fewer things we focus on. Perhaps only one main new thing we put in our "box" for the second half. That one thing will be our focus and our mission. This will make very clear what our "renaissance" could look like.

Inspired by my trip to Utah with five high school soccer players and many other youth trips similar to it, I have found what I want to focus my second half on are young people, particularly high school age through college students. Youth is what will be in my box.

Fun youth trip to the Smoky Mountains.

Now that I am 51 years old, I am a little over halfway to 100. I have always wanted to live to 100. It seems like those that make it that long are the ones who are mowing their own lawns at 97 or skiing at 95. That's the kind of old person I want to be. It will be interesting to see how my second half turns out.

What will help get me to 100 is spending more time in this great cause, focusing on speaking into the lives of young people around me. The challenge to lead and mentor them is what my aim will be. I am excited that I can choose to go after it. It charges my batteries just thinking about it.

I also encourage people to be intentional about making the second half of life the most impactful and meaningful part of their life. We don't want to just look behind us for happy times. We can be excited about our future and anticipate having some of our most memorable moments ahead of us. For me, it juices me up thinking about my future. There is so much to look forward to. So much that I can accomplish for good. So much growth that can occur in me and those around me. There is much to love about my future.

Throughout our lifetimes, we each go through numerous individual challenges that strengthen us, shape us, and mold our character. It's not only important, but it's also deeply fulfilling to discover how to make an impact with all we've learned, so it doesn't go to waste. This impact we can make should be in our box.

Questions to consider: If I am in my 40's, 50's, or 60's what is my second half going to look like? What will be the one thing in my box?

CHAPTER 13

Did I Tell Them?

"I will be generous with my love today. I will sprinkle compliments and uplifting words everywhere I go. I will do this knowing that my words are like seeds and when they fall on fertile soil, a reflection of those seeds will grow into something greater." —*Steve Maraboli*

I was excited to be in Chicago. It was one of my first times to visit, and the city looked amazing. I had come with my mother and some other ladies for a quick church related retreat. As a college student on break, it was fun even with the older crowd.

I was sharing a room with my mother in the hotel. I woke up tired the first morning to the sound of my mother in the shower—a reminder that it was time to get ready for the day.

I had heard that the motel provided a continental breakfast in the morning and that the breakfast would be hung on the doorknob of each room. After getting out of bed I walked directly to the door to get something to eat. I was starving and hoped it was some good stuff.

When I got to the door I was still in my underwear so I stealthily peeked out the door to look for our bag. When I did, I noticed that each door down the long hallway had a bag of food hanging from the knob. I quickly grabbed our bag and brought it inside. It wasn't much but it did have a big blueberry breakfast muffin, which was the kind I loved so much. My mother had already said she didn't want any breakfast so I gobbled it down pretty fast. It tasted awesome.

I was still craving more and instantly I thought of all the bags hanging on the doors. Would everyone really want theirs? It isn't really stealing is it? I had all sorts of thoughts go through my mind. But my stomach was still calling so I said to myself, "I am going to grab another one from off someone's door."

I went to the door and opened it just slightly to see if anyone was outside in the hallway. The coast was clear, so I darted across the hall to grab another bag. When I got the bag, I heard the door to my room snapped shut. That was the first moment I realized I had not thought through my plan very clearly. My stomach had overwhelmed my brain. I ran back to my door with my stolen food in hand and realized I had been locked out of my room without a key. Even worse, I had nothing but my underwear on. I was almost naked standing alone in the hallway of the hotel. I began to imagine one of my mom's friends opening her door to see me in all my glory.

I immediately started pounding on the door and yelled for my mom to open it. Unfortunately she was in the shower. I looked down at myself thinking what an idiot I was for getting greedy for the food. I said to myself, "Please don't let anyone see me like this." Still hearing the shower running, I panicked a bit. "How long could I be stuck out here?" I yelled for her more and kept pounding on the door. Finally to my delight, I heard my mom say, "What is going on out there?" I told her that I was locked out. She turned the shower off and got to the door as soon as she could. As soon as it opened I dashed in. I was so lucky to have no one see me. My mother looked at me in my underwear and said, "What in the world were you doing out there without your clothes on? I sheepishly held up the bag of food and said I was hungry. She laughed as I sat there feeling stupid.

I thanked her over and over that morning. Every once in a while, I realize how much I appreciate a person. That day, my mother saved me from a great deal of embarrassment. I was so thankful she was there. I really needed her. And, of course, not just that day, but throughout my life my mother has blessed me.

As I look back on my mother's impact I feel so fortunate to have her in my life. She is the rock, the foundation, and the base, to the character I possess today.

I sometimes wonder how much she realizes it. Unfortunately at the writing of this book she has had Alzheimer's for seven years. She has a slow progressing type. She still recognizes who I am but does not have the ability to answer normal simple questions. If I tell her a kind word today, she is impacted, but only briefly. Her short-term memory is basically gone.

A great night out with my mother at the very early stages of her Alzheimer's.

Sometimes I ask myself, did I tell her enough that I loved her? Did I tell her enough that she was my rock? Did I tell her enough what made her so special? I guess I won't know. I think I expressed my appreciation and love adequately, but I am sure I could have done more

One of my favorite quotes of all time is from Emerson. He said,

"I can't hear what you say because who you are rings so loudly in my ears." That concept speaks volumes about character, role models, parenting, and leadership. I believe this to be true, but can be taken too far. Some people use it as an excuse to not tell others how they feel about them. I have heard from many, "They know how I feel." That is a copout. I know grown adults who say, "If only my father would have told me he loved me." I see pain in their eyes as they verbalize it. What we say to others is very impactful. It is almost the icing on the cake to great character. When we can be authentic and express feelings to others without hesitation it is priceless.

I want to finish with a discussion about the effect of what we say to those around us. Words matter. What we say matters so much that it has lasting consequences on relationships. Whether good or bad, we remember what has been said to us, sometimes for the rest of our lives. Some people haven't spoken to family members for years because of an unkind word that was spoken. I still feel the sting of being told early in my career, "You are a bad salesman." Fortunately, it had a positive effect on my business life—It challenged me to work harder at my trade.

I have also received many positive words that impacted me. I will never forget the moment Tonya said, "yes" when I asked her to marry me. Where she said it and even the manner in which she said it I will never forget. Words matter.

So the life-lesson I see in this is: if we have something nice to say, we should say it. Affirming thoughts left unexpressed don't do anyone much good. We never know what kind of day someone may be having, or how much they might need an encouraging word, so it's important to give a compliment while it's fresh. Kindness makes a difference in our relationships, and affirmation makes a big difference to the person we share it with.

Professor Norihiro Sadato, research analyst and professor at the National Institute for Physiological Sciences in Japan, says, "To the brain, receiving a compliment is as much a social reward as being rewarded money. We've been able to find scientific proof that a person performs better when they receive a social reward after completing an exercise. Complimenting someone could become an easy and effective strategy to use in the classroom and during rehabilitation."

Members of Dr. Sadato's team described one of the experiments as follows: "We recruited 48 adults for the study who were asked to learn and perform a specific finger pattern (pushing keys on a keyboard in a particular sequence as fast as possible in 30 seconds). Once participants had learned the finger exercise, they were separated into three groups.

One group included an evaluator who would compliment participants individually; another group involved individuals who would watch another participant receive a compliment; and the third group involved individuals who evaluated their own performance on a graph.

When the participants were asked to repeat the finger exercise the next day, the group of participants who received direct compliments from an evaluator performed significantly better than participants from the other groups. The result indicates that receiving a compliment after exercising stimulates the individuals to perform better even a full day afterward."

Compliments not only help us perform better but they do much more. Particularly within the family, I see that complimenting openly and often is very critical to staying close. It is part of what deepens our relationships. Whether verbally and in writing, we can never express our appreciation and love too much. Recently I asked my wife, after 24 years of marriage what was her favorite present I have ever given her? She said it was the book I made for her telling her the "101 Reasons Why I Loved Her." It was a simple homemade book expressing the qualities and character traits I love about her. Just for fun, it also features a few cartoon drawings I made for her. It seems this book sticks out to her. It seems to have bonded us closer. We can never tell others enough how we feel. I want to be sure I don't miss future opportunities.

One of Tonya's favorite presents.

I think it was Mark Twain who said, "I can live for two months on a good compliment." I believe the reason affirmation impacts us so strongly is that we all face inner discouragements and gnawing self-doubts that long for relief. Heartfelt compliments are to the human soul what sun is to flowers. We all need the amazing warmth! We grow from them, and our relationships grow exponentially from honest expressions of our love and appreciation. With this in mind, I have included in the appendix a letter to each family member: sharing some of the strengths I see in them and reasons I love them. Of course, I try to tell them regularly how I feel, but my personal notes in the appendix are part of the legacy I hope they can always carry with them: to forever know many of the ways I love them.

A question to consider: How often do I tell those around me that I love them and WHY they mean so much to me?

Appendix

To Tonya,

Our Annual Halloween Party was only 15 minutes away. It had taken almost a week to decorate the downstairs, as well as put all the plastic down on the carpet to keep it from getting trashed. The food and the drinks were ready, Thriller was playing on the sound system, and the prep and planning that had taken weeks was finally coming to fruition.

We were in full costume once again. Tonya, this was your most important aspect of the party. We had to look legit. No last minute average costume. Your work has always been as professional as a Hollywood set. From the Internet, you had bought all the articles of clothing to the very last detail. Makeup and hair was specific to every character.

This year, I was to be Frankenstein and Brooke, Frankenstein's wife. You dressed up as Igor, and Grace was a miniature Frankenstein. We were almost completely ready. You had just finished placing oatmeal on your face to have a grotesque skin for your character. You then got some scissors to cut up your shirt to look more ragged. While cutting quickly, you accidentally sliced into your finger. Blood poured out quickly, as it was a deep cut. Fortunately, the red color all over didn't hurt your costume much because it was Halloween. People pay for that type of stuff.

The cut was bad enough that on a normal day we would have taken you to urgent care to get some stitches. But we were 15 minutes away from 100 people showing up to our house. There was no time for this. Stress was peaking from the pressure of a full week of hard work and from the urgency of the need to be ready for guests.

You frantically ran out of the bathroom to the kitchen. When you came back you had in your hand a small tube of Superglue. I would have never thought of it. You asked me to hold the skin together on your finger while you squeezed the glue onto the cut.

Amazingly it held. You quickly finished up the final touches to your makeup and it was picture time with the family. By the time the first person showed up, no one ever knew what you just went through. What they saw was the Shuleys once again in some great costumes for the party.

This situation personifies you so well. First, you are a hard worker. I have always called you the Energizer Bunny. You keep going and going and going… You are on the go from sun up to sun down. Even on the rare occasions when there is nothing going on, you won't sit and relax, you have to be doing something productive. Even though the Halloween party is a lot of work, we have had it 24 times. The energy it takes to pull it off has never deterred you from having it. Being the CEO of the household you continue feeding large numbers of people most Sunday's, buy the weekly groceries, volunteer at the school, keep a large house tidy, serve at the church, and take care of those in need. All this takes work and a lot of effort. Your energy is unmatched in our household. You have very little downtime. I have always been impressed by your work ethic. I am a hard worker myself, but sometimes I smile when I think: if I had had the same work intensity in my business it would have been dangerous.

Second, the costumes from our Halloween party illustrate the type of fun you create in our home. When friends arrive at the party and see us all dressed up it is rare that they don't break out laughing. This is you on a daily basis. You often make the kids laugh by your goofy looks, funny impressions, and crazy dancing. I find many times I can be sitting in our home in another area of the house and hear loud noises erupting which lead to craziness. You often laugh so hard it brings tears to your eyes. This is just normal for you. Laughter in the home is such a stress reliever. You are the main reason we have fun in our home.

A third feature about our parties that illuminates your character is that you always plan certain games for the little ones. You look to make sure everyone has a good time, and you arrange the games to reflect that. In life you have a heart for the forgotten, the ones that nobody seems to care about. I have noticed you feel more deeply than I do. You have more compassion than I, and you will go to great lengths to make sure those in need are taken care of. Weekly you come to me and say there is someone I needed to give some money to today, "They just needed it." or "I took this person to the hospital today because they are without a car." Sometimes these are inner city single moms that have no other way.

Not only do you take care of these people but they are some of your closest friends. You enjoy them and will often be found texting throughout the day. I find it rare to see a woman of your stature who has friendships in so many different social economic circles.

Fourth, even though we have over 100 friends attend our parties, the people you really feel most comfortable with are in our family. You love being around our kids. You can't get enough of them. Whether it is playing a game of horse, going shopping, playing soccer in the basement, or walking together through the beautiful local cemetery, you love being with your family. You don't watch from afar. You are right in the middle of it all, playing with them. There is no better moment for you than lying in a bean bag downstairs underneath a warm blanket, your kids lined up next to you in their own bean bags, the fire lit, lights dim, and a good movie playing on the screen. This is nirvana for you.

A fifth thing our Halloween parties reveal about you is that they are always fun for everyone but also clean and wholesome. We don't have crazy things going on that wouldn't be good for the whole family. You live that way yourself. You always try to do what's right and good. You have a pure heart. Because of this you are a good person with strong morals. You have spirituality about you that you don't wear on your sleeve but people just know. You work hard to do what's right and serve in the church and give your best. Whenever you do something wrong or we have a disagreement you always say, "I am sorry."

This annual party is one of my favorite family traditions. A sixth thing I love about you is that you do most of the work for the party and I get all the fun. I find this is much of what goes on in my life. You provide so much for me to be able to enjoy life. You take care of me in so many ways. I seem to get the glory for anything our family does but you are the one who does all the work and makes it happen. I love my life. Much of it is because you are in it and have executed on so many of my goals. You are the backbone of my dreams. Together we have had quite a life. I am so thankful for you and I love you deeply. After 24 years of marriage it is great to say I am totally in love. Can't wait to see the second half together!

Seventh, this party has music playing all night long. This is very much illustrative of you, who have brought music into our home since the day we got married. You play the piano and cello and simply have an ear for music. Because of you, everyone in our home plays an instrument (except me). There are so many times I am sitting around with little to do and I hear music in the home. It is you or one of our kids playing away. I love this. They are good at it too. One of my favorite things is to hear you and the girls sing in church together in a 3-part harmony. It is beautiful music. Having music in my life is one of the icings on the cake. My life is more full because of it. This is all thanks to you.

I am totally happy with the person you have become and accept you for who you are today. What I pray for you is to be happy and to love yourself as much as you love the kids and me. I pray for you to be healthy and to feel confident. I pray that you see a future so bright that you can't wait for it to come. I pray that you feel loved by me and all of our family. I pray that I can be the man who can be there for you for the rest of your life.

I sure love you Tonya. I will love you forever.

No one would know you sliced your finger badly 15 minutes before this picture was taken.

Our honeymoon in Kauai was one of my favorite weeks of my life. We were young and so in love. I have never regretted my choice to marry you.

My beautiful Tonya in Cabo.

You are always the fun and crazy one in the home.

I love to hike with you. We have seen some great scenes together.

We have had such a great adventures. I love this girl!

Traveling in Russia with my soul mate.

To My Oldest Son Ethan,

I was on the phone talking to a friend. It was a normal night in the young Shuley household. Tonya was in the kitchen fixing dinner. You were in the family room with me having a good time. At the age of two you could talk only a little bit, but boy were you active. We had bought you a Little Tikes basketball hoop to play with inside. In the previous couple of weeks, you had grown to love shooting the ball. The basket could be brought down to its lowest position, which was about 3 feet high. You would stand about 3 feet away and with a plastic ball, lift the ball up over your head, and throw it with two hands. If you made the shot, it would hit the stand on the way down and roll right back to your feet. I was proud of you because you picked it up so quickly. You could actually make most of your shots after only a short time playing.

That night, as I was on the phone, I watched you make so many baskets in a row I thought I should start counting the shots. You had already made many but I just started at one and counted each shot you made and how many you missed. You were automatic. I looked at you as the next Michael Jordan as I watched you hit 10 in a row, then another 10, then eight out of 10. I kept counting for what seemed a long while, until you reached 99 shots. At that point you had done enough and went to do something else. You had made 82 of the 99 shots all from around 3 feet away. I sat in amazement thinking about what I had just watched a two year old do. That seemed incredible knowing you had already made many shots before I started counting.

This personifies you in so many ways. First, how many kids can make so many shots in a row. What I have noticed with you is that you excel at everything you put your mind to. You not only participate in a variety of activities, but you seem to ACHIEVE much and be recognized for your achievements. You don't just do something; you always seem to make a splash at it. At the writing of this book, you are a college student. I can mention a few of your accomplishments. As a young child, you almost always scored the most on the soccer field. You were an Eagle Scout. You were the best drummer in your high school. You were a 7-time high school state champion runner. You went to Ukraine on his mission after high school and baptized more than most ever do in that country. You get almost straight A's in college. These things are achievements that other people might do, but few would stand out in their performance the way you do. You are a high achiever.

Second, how many two year olds could stand and take over 100 shots without losing interest? It took you probably 15 minutes to take that many shots. I don't see your drive in too many people. If you have a passion for something, others had better watch out. In high school when you wanted to get better at running, you went to all the regular running practices, then you would come home, eat dinner then walk over to the YMCA to swim for an hour. You just couldn't get enough workouts in a day. No one asked you to do this. When you do something, you don't just want to be good at it, you want to be great. You want to set records. You seem to want high achievement more than most people. Your drive is part of what makes you so great.

Third, your first word was "ball," not "mom" or "dad." You would look at that ball and stare at the design and color. You were curious. Years later, when you were in high school, we were sitting at the kitchen table eating dinner together and the doorbell rang. You hopped out of your seat and said, "I got it." You then answered the door, and a Japanese woman came in and walked with you right by the table, said "Hello," and kept walking into the study. You then shut the door. We looked at each other and said, "Who was that?" We had never seen her before. 45 minutes later you walked out the study with her and said goodbye.

When you walked back to the table, we asked who that was. You said she was your Japanese teacher. This apparently was your third lesson with her. You had never told us you wanted to learn the Japanese language, nor that you had adult women in our home teaching you. You had used your own money and never told us about it. We were amazed. What high school student on top of your normal classes wants to add a language class of that difficulty? You love languages, but also love to learn about a wide variety of interests. You are curious about the world. Because of this, we took you on your graduation trip to Japan so that you could experience the culture there. You are always listening to podcasts, and/or reading on the Internet about various subjects. You are a smart person who can explain facts from the history of the waterbed to the details of Russian versus the Japanese language. You are an extremely smart person and quite interesting to talk to.

Fourth, when we first got the Little Tikes hoop I sat and showed you the best way to throw the ball with two hands to make a basket. You learned very quickly and went with it. In life I have found you to be very teachable. You are definitely very opinionated, but at the end of the day you listen to your parents and take our advice. It is a great virtue to be teachable. Whether it is advice on dating, overcoming sports injuries, spiritual guidance, advice on money, etc.., you really seem to listen and treat our advice as wisdom. As parents, it is a blessing in our lives.

A fifth thing I admire about you is your ability to act on faith. It takes faith in yourself to make a shot. You have to believe it will go in before it does. At a very young age, you have been diligent and faithful in trying to follow what Tonya and I have suggested is best for you. Sometimes things that you were not even sure you believed, yourself, but as a youth you did what was asked, because we thought it best for you. Dieter Uchtdorf once said, "It is your choices that show who you truly are, far more than your abilities." Ethan, you have shown a lot of faith in your parents' wisdom. Even with things you didn't quite understand. You seem to want to always try to do what is right. As you have gotten older that foundation has allowed you to explore much more of what you believe for yourself. I am so thankful for the trust that you have put in us. It is a blessing as a parent.

Sixth, you have led the way for the rest of your siblings. As parents we learn a lot from our first go at parenting. We tend to make the most mistakes on the first child. You are the only child we ever tested out spanking. We stopped pretty quickly. You were the only one of our children impacted by having to change schools. You were the only child for a few things. Yet you were able to set a good example for the rest of your siblings. You always did well in school, you excelled in sports, you didn't complain about going to church, you made friends with good kids, which allowed us to have a high level of trust in you when you were a teenager. You made the decision to serve a mission for the church. Additionally, you went to college, which also set a high standard for the siblings who follow. We are very fortunate to have you set such a great example for your brother and sisters.

I am totally happy with the person you have become and accept you for who you are now. What I pray for in your future is for you to see yourself as I see you; just a terrific person with a ton to offer to others, full of confidence. I pray for you to put Jesus first in your life, so that all your decisions are based on the person and the principles of Christ. I pray you see your life directed by God, even when things are not going your way. I pray for you to have a constant desire to serve others and make the burdens of others lighter. I pray for you to be blessed with a loving wife and children to raise. I also pray for you to find a career that is a fit for you so you can make a difference and enjoy the ride while providing for your family. And of course, I pray that you will always want to come home to see the parents because it is a safe place where you know you are loved.

I sure love you Ethan. I will love you forever!

You never got tired of the Little Tikes hoop

Cutest baby picture I have ever seen.

You always showed such confidence on the soccer field.

*The fight to the finish at the Kentucky State 1600-meter final.
One of many state championships.*

Graduation trip to Japan fascinated Ethan.

To My Son Blake,

The game couldn't have been closer. It was the semi finals of the regional high school soccer playoffs. Highlands was playing against its archrival, Covington Catholic. They had gone on to win the state championship a few times in the previous years and always stood between us and the state tournament. This year it was different. Our defense was stout. Few teams had the ability to score on us and this game was illustrating some of our best strengths. Blake, as one of the captains of the soccer team, you had always played your heart out. The game had finished the overtime period without a result. Now it came down to penalty kicks. Each team had five players who would alternate kicking a penalty shot, and the most goals scored out of five would win. This was a high-pressure situation. The teams picked their best players to come to the line. But many times the pressure would make a player miss the goal and shake their head in disgust.

The first player of both teams missed their first shot. Then you got up there and calmly placed your shot low and to the left corner of the goal for a score. The pressure got to most of the others, and players on both sides missed shots, so the score was two shots a piece after five. Then, in the second round of shots, it was sudden death. The 7th Highlands player made his shot and Covington Catholic missed. After that final save, your team went crazy jumping, screaming, and hugging each other with joy. Some of you dog piled on top of each other with your hands held high yelling, "We won." In the crowd, as parents, we were high fiving each other, so happy for our kids. It was the biggest victory of your high school experience. You will never forget it.

Details about this experience represent many things that personify you. First, you are a very confident person. You have learned to be confident under pressure, as well. Prior to your senior year, though, you were not like that. In high school you and I played a lot of ping-pong together. It was a way we could connect, talk, and have fun together without any distractions. If I ever wanted to talk to you about anything I would ask you to play ping-pong. It always led to good conversions.

But when we kept score, which wasn't often, and you had me on the ropes close to game point, even if I was behind by a few points I would find a way to win. I felt like I could get into your head. You had never beaten me, until one day in your senior year it happened. I couldn't mess with you enough and you won. From then on something changed in your head, you beat me many times. I remember telling you that your confidence in ping-pong was going to cross over onto the soccer field. When you stood at the ball for the penalty shot, you were the most confident player on the field that day. Your mind was in the right place, simply calm and cool. Since then I have seen your confidence in many ways: on your mission among other missionaries, dating girls, and interacting with family. I mentioned earlier that confidence is the number one driver of success. Blake, you will be successful in life.

A second thing this regional playoff game illustrates to me about you is your style. At the soccer game, you were in the school uniform with the captain's armband. You just looked cool. You looked like a stud out there. One thing I love about you is you have always had style. Whether it was when you were young and you dressed up like a Major League Baseball player, or dressed in nice clothes for high school, or got the fade cut for your hair before going on a date, you always have style.

I also respected you for starting up a shoeshine business in my firm's office. When you were in high school you met many of my colleagues and shined their shoes with a seven-step process. They looked perfect every time. You, of course, got to know all of the name brand shoes and learned to converse with everyone coming in or out of my office.

The third thing I saw about you relative to this playoff game is your ability to connect with others. That game certainly bonded your teammates together. This was a team win and you loved each other. Blake, you have always been one to bring people together. You are quite a leader. People want to be around you. You are comfortable with your friends and display a no judgment attitude. When you were young, you always got your friends to come over and play at the house. As a teenager it didn't stop. You would have sleepovers with about six friends from school. They would never get together unless you made it happen. But they had a blast when it did. The sleepovers consisted of indoor aggressive basement soccer, FIFA gaming at a high level, a large amount of food, swimming in the pool, and no drama at all. We always felt comfortable with your choice of friends. I know your friends can't wait for you to come back from your mission because, of course, they haven't all gotten together since you left.

Fourth, you love your mother. You have a sense of compassion for your parents but a soft spot for women. You can learn a lot about a person by how he treats his mother. Blake, you have always been very gentle and kind to Tonya. In a good way, you just seem to be more sensitive than most. You will cry occasionally when you are sad. You will listen, when others are feeling amiss. This wasn't always the case. As a young boy you used to obliterate Brooke at every opportunity. One time, after hitting her in the face with a plastic baseball bat, you came running in to say that Brooke was hurt. When we saw blood all over her face, we asked you what had happened. You immediately said, "I hit her in the face with the bat." You responded with no remorse as if it was totally normal. We laugh at it now because of how much you feel for others today.

Fifth, often while you cleaned the dishes, you would turn on your music and dance behind the sink while you washed. The music could have been almost any genre. You had the largest array of music of anyone I know. Whether it was pop, country, rap, love songs, or even old classics, you had it on your playlist. Many nights, a dance party would erupt in the kitchen. On numerous drives home, we would sing at the top of our lungs to "My Way" by Frank Sinatra. You have a way of relaxing everyone to the point that their inhibitions are swept away. By the end of the night, everyone is singing and dancing. You just love music and you have made it fun for everyone. I just love that about you.

Sixth, in that penalty box, I knew you would make that kick. Your mindset had grown so strong during your high school years that I didn't worry about it. You have always been a child that I haven't really worried much about. Everything hasn't always gone as planned but you just seem to stay on the straight and narrow path. I have always trusted you completely.

Heck, I even let you drive my Tesla on a date. There just is a foundation you have that keeps you moving in the right direction. I don't worry about your financial future, I don't worry about you being a great husband and father, I don't worry about you losing your faith, I just don't worry about you. How nice that is as a parent! I know you will be successful in everything you really care about. Not in some flashy way. You will just quietly get there.

Related to your solid mental foundation, a seventh thing I love about you is your wisdom in following rules. In the penalty box of a soccer game, the ball must be placed exactly over the mark and the player must wait till the ref blows the whistle for the shot to be taken. You knew the rules of the game like the back of your hand. You have always been good at knowing what needs to be done and following the rules. It comes very natural to you. Also, you are of strong moral character and are an example to many by the way you live. You get this from being faithful to God's commandments without question. This applies to many areas of your life.

When instructed at work, you work hard and do exactly what is asked of you. You will be very successful in your career because of your ability to do what is expected of you. On your mission in Brazil where many of the other missionaries have had a hard time following the rules, you rose above the best you could to obey the mission rules even when they didn't want to. You to be obedient pushed many which moved the work forward. Your ability to follow the rules will bless your life a great deal. I am so happy that you have the gospel in your life, which will give you the playbook to follow for experiencing the most joy through your life's journey.

What I pray for you is to have a chance to influence many. I pray that you will have the courage to be a leader among men. I pray that you will not wait for opportunities to come to you but you will direct your life and seek after your dreams. One of my favorite phrases in life is, "It never hurts to ask." I pray that you will put yourself out there and ask over and over again for what is needed to reach your dreams. I pray you will always have a humble confidence about asking and that your requests will find favor. I pray that you will find your passion for your future career. I pray that you will never forget your mother. You have always treated her so well, and I hope that always continues. It is so important to her.

I sure love you Blake. I will love you forever!

As captain of the Highlands soccer team, you were very confident in your senior year.

You could always be found juggling balls of all types. The Outer banks family reunion provided plenty of space.

You always look so stylish. There is a reason you were once asked to model an underwear line.

You have a way of making nature feel spiritual.

You love to hike. What a picturesque way to start the 18 mile Icelandic hike.

You seem to find the most amazing scenes the world has to offer.

To My Daughter Brooke,

The Joshua trees are quite unique. In the National Park they are everywhere. They grow to be over 20 feet tall and look half tree and half cactus. It is one of the different types of impressive scenes California has to offer.

We had traveled to Palm Springs to visit my father for spring break and took a day to hike the park. Our family had hiked through the desert for a couple miles and came to a section that looked like a 200 foot rock pile shaped like the top of an ice cream cone.

You and I looked at each other and said, "Should we scramble to the top?" My dad and some others were not up for it but you and I thought we had to get to the top. Everyone else took a break and we were off.

Climbing to the top was a challenge. There was no trail. The tan colored rock was formed with a gritty texture that would scratch a person pretty unpleasantly if he or she happened to trip and slide on it. However, the rock was composed of large boulders that could be scrambled up somewhat handily.

You were up for the challenge. The strength in your legs almost made the climb easier for you than it was for me. But I was blessed with longer arms and legs to reach certain spots. As we climbed up, looking for a doable path at every turn we slowly made it towards the top. We helped each other up the big boulders but you mainly handled it on your own.

When we finally made it to the top we got a little nervous with the drop offs. But we were so proud of ourselves. It was such a good feeling to conquer it on such a pretty day. We were not in Kentucky any more.

At the top we took a few photos, waved to the family and then started to make our way down. As a father I love these one-on-ones with my kids. You and I enjoyed the adventure of finding a way up and down. When we reached the bottom, the rest of the family asked how hard it was because they had watched us the whole time and could see some of the big boulders we'd had to maneuver to somehow get up over. They were impressed. We gave each other a high five and continued on our hike.

Brooke, this scramble up the rock pile personifies you in so many ways. First, you can handle physically hard challenges. You are a tough girl. Your toughness may be partly due to the roughhousing you experienced with your older brothers in childhood play. You always took it nicely and didn't cry much. Your pain tolerance has always been high. You were the only child who when we pulled your teeth you did not whine or cry at all. Your eyes watered from the pain but you really didn't react at all. I still remember being so impressed with your control.

When we went on hikes that were hard, the boys would try something and you would follow. When they would slide down a steep snowfield, you would go next. When they jumped off a cliff into the water, you jumped right behind. If the boys went on a 10 mile hike, you did too. You always seemed to feel that you could do what they did. This simply made you tough. One day when you are married, this will go a long way for you as a mother.

The second thing this rock climb exemplifies to me about you is your willingness to go for new challenges, and your humble surprise at what you accomplish. For example, at the beginning of the rock pile, we both wondered if we really could get all the way up. It looked almost impossible in spots. Then we found ourselves at the top saying how did we get here? I find your life has been similar to this. You have surprised yourself over and over again at the things you are able to do. At this point I would place no limits on your ability, because you are still reaching heights deemed not possible in many different areas of your life. I have seen you begin to play and sing guitar, then you find yourself singing the National Anthem at a professional soccer game in front of 22,000 people. How did you get to this point? I have seen you as a defender on the freshman high school soccer team, then go to striker on the JV team and end up being voted the team's Most Valuable Player of the Year. How did you get there? I have seen you begin running a couple of miles a day for a health class then find herself running a half marathon in high school. How did you get there? You just find yourself regularly doing things that at one point in time were seemingly impossible. It is fun to watch.

A third thing the rock climb typifies about you is your conversational style. Climbing up the rocks, we talked the whole time. You put me at ease when we talk because you are so nice and have no guile. I saw this at an early age in the way you treated your younger sister. You just loved Grace and were always nice to her. In high school you were great friends, partly because of your kindness. I always tell my kids that it is "nice to be nice." You personify that so well. We need more of that in the world.

A fourth thing I love about you is your serenity. That is what I felt with you as we were looking over the Joshua Tree National Park perched on the top of our climb—a serenity that was almost spiritual. Brooke, you are one that feels that peace. Spiritually, you have never been one to doubt things. It seems you have faith to know Truth without having to question every little thing. You just believe. Your consistency in your beliefs has helped you make good choices. You have stayed away from things that will lead you down the wrong path. You have maintained high moral standards. In high school when some of your closest friends have abandoned clean living, you have chosen to be bored and lonely at times on the weekends versus succumbing to worldly values. That is true strength.

When we got to the top of the rocks we, of course, had to take a few pictures for Instagram. As I captured a few photos, I thought you looked simply pretty and athletic. That is the fifth thing I love about you. I have always thought of you as a beautiful child. With your blue eyes and blond wavy hair you are simply stunning. You have a few talents in the beauty arena. I have never met a girl at such a young age that knows how to do hair like you do. At junior prom in high school you started a small business and charged $20 per person to get their hair ready for the night. You had four random girls respond from Instagram and ask you. They looked beautiful from your touch. You also have a sense of fashion. With you and your mother's talents in shopping, you know how to dress. From a casual day to a formal event, you are always in style. What's most important is to be beautiful inside which is what I am most impressed about with you. You have both; beauty on the inside and out.

A sixth thing I love about you is your ability to relax. When we got to the top of the rocks, we took the opportunity to sit and relax. It had been a strenuous, challenging climb. And you know how to relax! It is not uncommon to come home from work and find you nestled in a beanbag, under a blanket, writing in your journal, sitting next to the fire. It almost looks like a scene from a Hallmark movie. You have always had a busy life but when you get done with something and have a moment you know how to take advantage of it. When we built a pool a few years ago, no one has taken advantage of the peace and tranquility of the pool like you have. You particularly love the summer! It is your time to relax. That is where you get your zen moments. I find some people in life do not know how to recharge their batteries very well on a consistent basis. I do not worry about that at all with you. You will be a pro.

What I pray for you is that you will be confident around all sorts of people. I pray that you will always be yourself, regardless of the crowd. What a great personality to share. I pray that you will see how much of a leader you are. I pray that you will jump actively at any opportunity to serve others. I pray that you will find a spouse who will treat you in the manner of which you are worthy. I pray that you will always make the gospel the center of your life.

I sure love you Brooke. I will love you forever!

At the top of Joshua Tree National Park's random rock pile.
It took some doing to get to the top.

From birth you have always been a beautiful girl!

Playing at your first paying gig. Fun night.

You have always had style. Especially with Delicate Arch reflecting in your cool shades.

You know how to relax and there is no place better than our pool.

To My Daughter Grace

One day we heard you crying in your room. You couldn't stop crying. We didn't know what was wrong. But you just kept sobbing. After what seemed like 30 minutes we found out that a middle school friend of yours had just suddenly died. Lilliana was a cheerleader, a spunky, friendly girl who had had quite a few classes with you. After a cheerleading competition, she had felt very sick and had been taken to the hospital where she died. It was caused by a strep infection that had come from nowhere.

You and the rest of our community in Fort Thomas were devastated. You were only in 8th grade, which makes it very difficult to wrestle with such a loss. On Monday the first day back to class the middle school kids were a mess. Basically each period of the day all the kids just cried with each other. It was a day of mourning. It was dramatic and hard. No schoolwork was done that day. Everyone was just trying to get through the day.

When you got home you were totally exhausted. You were physically and emotionally drained to the core. So much so, that we decided to keep you home the following day just to rest and not be part of all the chaos that would probably continue the next day.

I stayed home that day because we had some out of town family visiting. We did our best to cheer you up and have a better day. We planned on going out to eat for lunch but you decided you wanted to stay home. We would only be gone for an hour. So we gave you some alone time.

When we came back home from lunch we found that you had decided to write a song for Lilliana. You did it for her but I am sure it was therapeutic for yourself. You played it on the piano. It was titled, "Lilliana." As we listened to the lyrics and the melody we all cried. It was beautiful. It was emotional and so touching. We couldn't believe you had done this in one short hour.

As we listened to this, my first thought was that Lilliana's family needed to hear it. It would mean something to them. So I called a friend in the community to see how I could connect with the family. We had not previously met them. When I shared the song with my friend she suggested that the entire community which was hurting so badly, really needed to hear this. She asked if I could forward the song to a few friends.

I thought it would be easiest to post it on YouTube so then it could be forwarded. So I asked you to play the song and I videoed it on my phone. You played it perfectly. We then posted it on YouTube and sent it to this friend. She passed it along to a few friends.

Then what happened next was something we had not foreseen. It started to go viral throughout the community. It went from 100 views to 3,000 within minutes. By the end of the first night you had over 10 thousand views. Before it all calmed down, you had over 30 thousand views. It truly impacted the community and most importantly it affected Lilliana's family. Her father reached out to me to express thanks and asked if you would join some of Lilliana's closest friends and sing your song at the funeral.

The day of the funeral the lines were packed for the viewing and then the funeral was filled to capacity. Grace, you were strong and played the song without breaking down. Luckily it was at the beginning of the funeral. Had it been after a couple talks, who knows if you could have done it.

I was so proud of you for your impact and how you didn't want any notoriety; you just wanted all the focus to be on Lilliana. It was quite a tribute. It was quite a proud moment for such a great daughter of mine.

This experience personifies my Gracie. First, you feel deeply for others. I find that most people do, but your level of feeling is very deep. You feel it to the core. That is a great thing. It is also a burden. Being that empathetic allows your days to be affected by how others are doing. But overall I love this about you. You show your emotions. You can cry, laugh, joke, be serious, and express feelings. This has always helped you have good friends, filled with love for each other. In our family, when Ethan left on his mission it was very difficult for you. You missed him terribly. That was the day you began writing songs. It was an escape for you to deal with your emotions. You struggled with his distance because you cared so deeply. Not everyone is that way. But you get so much out of relationships that this is a very positive trait.

A second quality this song illustrates about you is your talent. You wrote the song for Lilliana in an hour. How did you do this? You are one of the most talented people I have ever met. You have some of the best dance moves; yet have taken very few dance classes. You sing like an angel. You can play multiple instruments. You can act on stage and get into character extremely well. If I ask you to create a tear in your eye you can do it on the spot. You are wicked smart at school. You are one of the best writers I know. Whether it is lyrics in a song or a short story, you are way above your age in ability. Your recall is amazing which makes tests in school much easier for you than for others. Athletically, you were captain of the freshman soccer team. I remember as a 5th grader you wanted to make top five in the mile run to win a turkey right before Thanksgiving. You trained for a week and then of course took 5th, coming home with the prized turkey. I could go on. Your talents are numerous and you will be recognized years to come for your abilities.

Third, you are one of the funniest people I know. You just have a humorous personality. You can speak with almost every language accent. Whether it is imitating Jacque Clouseau or using your English accent as Aunt Spiker in James and the Giant Peach, you have us all laughing. Then there are your funny facial expressions that can take us in any direction. We have seen many since your early childhood days. You definitely keep us on our toes.

Fourth, when you were feeling sad about Lilliana, you decided that day to do something about it. You wrote a song to help you express your grief. It was therapeutic to your healing. You took a step to deal with your emotions. I view this as a great characteristic. The other day you were sad because you were not invited to a going away party for a friend. You thought you shouldn't have been left out. Because you feel so deeply and are emotional you cried about it for a bit, but after you collected yourself you texted your friends to express your feeling that there were elements of your friendship that everyone needed to work on. Your friends all responded positively and the drama was over. People often hold in their emotions and do not pursue a healthy outlet to express them. Then, negative feelings build up inside until bottled emotions eventually come out in a big explosion. Grace, you have become good at expressing how you feel through music, discussions with friends, and many other ways. Frankly you just deal with it. That will help you so much in family life in the future. It is a great personality trait that I love about you.

Fifth, that song you wrote was simple and beautiful. That is partly why so many people were touched and it went viral. Well, there is much that is beautiful about you. Physically you have gorgeous brown, highlighted, flowing, thick hair that every girl dreams of. You have a smile that melts a father to the core. The first time I saw you dressed up for the homecoming dance in high school, you were wearing a fancy dress and eye make up for the first time. You looked like a woman. I saw your date all buzzed thinking he had the best date that night. I just thought to myself, 'Oh no. This girl is all grown up now!' It's a scary thing for a dad.

Sixth, when you wrote that song it expressed purity in love for a classmate. The song became a way everyone could express their love for Lilliana. Your beauty isn't just on the outside. On the inside you have a spirit about you that just wants to be Christ like. You want to express His love in everything you do. Your life, to me, represents love in many ways. The way you give such great hugs. When you hug me, you don't have any stiffness about it. You wrap both arms around me and squeeze with everything you have. I have always taught that a real hug is with two arms and lasts at least seven seconds. Some people have rolled their eyes at that suggestion, but you have no problem with it. You give a long, strong hug and finish it off with a soft kiss on the cheek. I will never get tired of that affection from my daughter.

Grace, as my youngest child, you have often benefited from favorable treatment from your siblings. But you have returned that with a thankful heart and deep love coming back to them. You are very close to them. In John 13:34-35 Jesus says, "A new commandment I give unto you, that ye love one another; as I have loved you, that ye also love one another. By this shall

all men know that ye are my disciples, if ye have love one to another." You are a disciple of Jesus.

I pray for you that you will look forward to the future anticipating it to be a bright fulfilling life. I pray you reach every big dream you have for yourself. I pray that you will always be honest with yourself and others. I pray you will lead those around you to a better life. I pray that you will learn how to pray regularly and receive Godly answers to life's questions. I pray you will practice good health throughout your life. I pray you will love yourself as much as I do. I pray you will use all of your many talents to make a difference in this world.

I sure love you Grace. I will love you forever!

From day one you came out fun. We had to wrap you in duct tape to keep you from taking your clothes off at night.

You have always had love toward animals.

You played Aunt Spiker in James and the Giant Peach.
Your humor and accent stole the show.

Recording the song dedicated to the life of Lilliana.
It went viral touching many in the community.

Captain of the freshman soccer team.

The night of your first High School Homecoming Dance.

To My Dad

Coming home for the summer was always a nice break from the schoolwork. During my college days I always came home at that time. It was this time of my life when you started to hit it big at work. Your income had always been above average but now it seemed we were living a different lifestyle.

One summer, I came home to see that you had purchased a new bright red Mercedes 500SL convertible. It was beautiful and fast. I especially enjoyed driving with you on a summer day with the top down and the wind blowing through my hair. It was a very free feeling. I couldn't think of a nicer sports car for you to own.

One night, you and I headed out in the car to go downtown to a Reds baseball game. It would be the start of a great night. The night was warm; the wind was blowing through my hair as we drove over the bridges into Cincinnati. I hadn't been to a Reds game yet, and this year they were winning their division with hopes of the playoffs. It couldn't get much better than this.

You had season tickets in the blue section 10 rows back behind home plate. As we walked down to our seats I felt like royalty. It was two rows away from the Reds managers wives. The jewelry on those ladies was something to be seen. We were in the "Who's Who" section of the stadium.

After we sat down, you and I talked, ate some junk food, and enjoyed a great baseball game. That year the Reds had all the stars like Barry Larkin, Chris Sabo, and Eric Davis. They had pitchers like Tom Browning and a trio of closers called "The Bad Boys." They would go on to sweep the Oakland A's in the World Series.

That night they had a close game with a division foe, which made the stadium alive. You and I were on the edge of our seats for every pitch. In the last inning, the batter hit a base hit to win the ball game. The crowd erupted in cheers. We went crazy. People were out of their seats for a while, as the fireworks blasted off signaling the win. We had such a fun time being there! We both loved sports and appreciated when the teams were great. We didn't have any deep conversation that night, but we enjoyed commenting on the game and on various other things going on in each other's lives. I have always remembered that game. It is one of my fondest memories with you.

That night was so fun. When I think of you, immediately what comes to mind is that you are a fun person. I have always respected you for that. You have been the person in the family who wouldn't sit around. You have to be doing something. Your life always includes fun in it. Whether it was playing golf on the links, watching a sporting event, or going out to dinner, there certainly is fun in your day. It bred into our family in a big way and I feel if there is any sense of fun in me I got it from you.

I asked you last year, now that you are in your mid 70's what your goals are for the next 10 years. You told me, "I just want to have fun with my life. That will require good health." Your goal is to have fun. You are currently doing a great job at that.

A second thing that game represents to me about you is that you have worked hard at your career and now you can enjoy the fruit of your labor. The seats at the game were not cheap, but you had earned the money to afford them. You worked very hard throughout your life and had some bumps and bruises with your career, but you rose above your circumstances and became a leader in your industry. You came from nothing financially but made a name for yourself and became very secure. You have been a great example to me of thinking big about what I can accomplish with my career and being wise with the money that I make. I believe I am debt free because of the financial discussions I have had with you over the years. Your career and financial strength are something I have always wanted to emulate.

A third reason that game is memorable to me is that it represents the way you spent time with your children. You loved watching the Reds. You loved watching us as well. I have always felt supported and loved by you. You seemed to be at every big race of mine in high school. When I went on a mission, you totally supported my decision emotionally and financially. Even with different beliefs in certain areas, you have never criticized or made me feel like I shouldn't be myself. I have appreciated that support throughout my life. I feel like whatever I do, you will always love me. What a super feeling.

I sure love you dad. I will love you forever!

You were a sharp looking young man, who from a small logging town became a national business leader.

Even with your busy schedule you still made it a focus to support me in what I was involved in.

To My Mom

I was nervous sitting in my seat on the plane. Everyone else had already left, but I sat there anxious to get off. Because of my church mission I hadn't seen my family in two years. My time away had been an awesome experience, but now the moment had come to see my family again and start the next chapter of my life.

As I got up out of my seat, I placed a Santa Claus stocking cap on my head and began the walk. It was December 23rd so I wore that hat knowing I would be the best Christmas present you would get that year. You had put your Christmas tree up on November 7th because you knew once it was up I would be home very soon.

When I walked off the plane, there you were, my family standing there, with Laura's boyfriend videotaping the whole scene. You were the first to walk up to me and hug me tight. We didn't let go for over a minute, which allowed us to cry some happy tears. I had missed you. I loved you so much that, for months on my mission trip, I had an irrational fear of you dying while I was gone. Well, you weren't dead. That was over now. We were together again, and it felt like home.

It was a great time of year to arrive home. The whole family was available because everyone was off work and around for Christmas. It was so nice to catch up on everyone's life. A lot had happened in the family over the two years that I had been gone.

Christmas morning was funny. I had been in a suit and tie for two years and basically had no clothes to wear for college. My mission life has conditioned me to not be worldly at all, so I figured I would need very little. But that was not what you had in mind. You had shopped and shopped for me. Then you shopped some more. That morning as I began opening presents it got crazy. Each present would have four to five shirts or four to five pants in the box. Then I received shoes, suits, and the works. The pile of opened gifts dwarfed everyone else's. I received so much. I literally began to feel guilty as I continued to open presents. It just wasn't expected.

You were just that way. You really wanted to take care of me and make sure I had everything I needed for the next phase of my life. You wanted me to look good for the girls when my dating life would begin again. You had good fashion sense and it was in full display.

I have always felt that you have a special place in your heart for me. You just loved me and could always relate to me. We have had a bond that is especially pronounced because of our similar view of the gospel. When I was growing up, we had many private discussions of a spiritual nature that I don't think you could have with others. Our relationship has always been a safe place for both of us.

This brings me to the first reason I love my mom. I know you are going to heaven. I just know it. You are not a perfect person, but you are one that has strived to do what's right your whole life. You have relied on the Lord for everything. You have dealt with many difficulties but have never wavered in your faith nor doubted God in any way. You have done so, even under the criticism from your parents. You have served the less fortunate and have never given up on certain people, even when you weren't getting much back in return. You have learned how to forgive and have been blessed to be happier because of it. You are truly my role model for gospel living. I want to live my life in a way so that I will be in the same place after this life as you will be. You deserve all that God has in store for those who follow Him.

A second thing I especially love about you is the way you show love. When I walked off the plane that day, one thing I knew for sure was that you loved me. You showed it in the way you hugged me. You showed it to me on my mission by calling me on the phone occasionally, even though it was against our mission rules at the time. You said you missed me so much, you couldn't help yourself. There is something that creates great inner confidence when we feel truly loved by others. I had that, growing up in my household and it never stopped. It wasn't shown in any unique way. But I have always felt it in abundance. Even though you suffer from dementia today, you still look at me as if I am the most important person in the world to you. Even without much memory, you still state every time we are together just how much you love me. You show it in your eyes by the way you look at me.

A third characteristic I love about you is that you always put family first. When I came home from my mission, you wouldn't have wanted to be anywhere else in the world. You wanted to be with your family. That has always been your priority from day one. Your decisions have always been based on faithfulness to family.

I was in middle school the year you and dad separated. That Christmas, you only had $43 to spend on gifts for us kids. You swallowed your pride and asked some friends to help make the Christmas cheer spread a little wider for us. You wanted life to feel as normal as possible under the circumstances. Of course, we knew none of this at the time, but you didn't get anything, yourself, for Christmas. I don't remember us kids being thoughtful at our young age to give you a gift so you just went without. That didn't seem to matter to you, as long as the kids were happy.

Later in life you dedicated yourself to genealogy research to understand your family history. You loved this. You valued understanding your roots. You even spent time publishing a book regarding your family history. This was important and something you truly enjoyed.

Your life has always been dedicated to your family. I have tried to emulate this when I have options for personal fun or business decisions. If I put it through the lense of "What's best for the family," then I have done what my mother has done.

I sure love you Mom. I will love you forever!

Mom, you were a beautiful young lady.

*Even while you were on your mission you have always
been up to do anything that sounded fun.*

To My Older Brother Mike

It was a Saturday afternoon and I had been on my bike for 8 hours. Training runs of 150 miles take forever. I had ridden part of the first 100 miles to Rabbit Hash Kentucky and back with a friend. Then I rode the last 50 miles with another friend on the roads around my house. The humidity and sun had worn me out completely. But I was now ready for the Lotoja Race that would be held in 3 weeks. Training was complete.

The Lotoja is a one-day 206 mile cycling race from Logan Utah to Jackson Hole Wyoming. It traverses over three mountain passes before ending in one of the most beautiful towns in America.

I had done the race twice before. I knew what it took to make it to the finish. It was all the preparation leading up to the race. The block of training in the last month required two 120 mile rides and a 150 miler. That, plus all the other rides was a large sacrifice for the family and myself. I was out on the road alone for many hours throughout the week.

This year you and I were both doing it. You lived in Utah so we couldn't train together. But we both loved cycling and were excited about the race.

That morning we had our friends, who were our support crew, take us to the starting line. I had a goal of winning my division. That year you entered the race with the desire to finish it for the first time. We both were excited to get this race started.

The first 45 miles are rather flat. But then the first mountain pass hits. It is a gradual twenty-mile pass that tips upward to the peak, especially in the last 5 miles. I was hitting it hard going up the pass. In the final mile of the climb I realized that I didn't have what it took and I got dropped. It was a depressing feeling because when that happened I knew I could never catch back up. My goal for the race was already over.

Now I was just riding to finish strong. I had done so well in the previous year that I knew I would be behind that time. My motivation started to diminish, as I also felt more tired than normal. The second mountain pass hit and I was crawling up the mountain with very little strength.

After coming back down and riding up a canyon toward the final mountain I felt horrible. My back hurt, my legs were dead, I felt sleepy from a lack of good sleep that week, it was just not my day. I was riding only 18 miles per hour, which was a normal easy pace, but I couldn't even hang on to a group as they rode away from me.

At that point I said to myself, 'What is all of this for?' I had sacrificed so much of my time and my family's time. I said out loud, 'I did all of that for this?' At that point I burst out crying. I just lost it. I couldn't believe I had wasted so much time of my life for such a disappointing outcome.

I was fortunate I had sunglasses on so that spectators couldn't see me crying like a baby. Eventually I made it over the final mountain. I had nothing to ride for, so I went down the other side and arrived at the aid station, which was 120 miles into the race. I told my support crew friend that I was done. I cried again.

After being consoled for a bit, I was able to pack my bike in his car and we rode to the next aid station around 150 miles into the race. I thought I would wait there to watch you come by. You had been behind me about an hour or so.

After riding in the car and waiting at the 150 mile aid station I noticed that I really wasn't that tired anymore. A thought came to my mind. Maybe I can ride with you the last 56 miles. Your pace was slightly slower so I thought my legs would be all right. Maybe I can help pull you to the finish.

So when you showed up at the station I was ready to go. It was fun. We rode together as brothers. You were having a great race. You felt strong and thought you could make it to the finish for the first time but still had the last 50 miles to go.

We talked, and rode in the small peloton. I lead the group for much of the time, trying to pull you in. My legs were back and I felt comfortable. I really enjoyed helping you achieve your goal of breaking 12 hours. It was fun to achieve this together. It felt like a bonding moment out on the road.

As we approached the city of Jackson a thought came to me. This horrible race had turned into something great. Lemons had turned into lemonade. You stayed strong through the finish and we both rode through the finish line together. It was quite a moment that I will never forget. One of the best experiences I have ever had with you. We both made it to Jackson!

This experience with you personifies you in a few ways. First, while we rode we talked with each other and also conversed with the other riders. There was solid camaraderie all the way to the finish. Mike, you have a way of making everyone comfortable. There is not a stranger you couldn't walk up and talk to for the next 30 minutes. You would enjoy it. There is no judgment, no agenda. You just keep your guard down and so does everyone else. I feel it is a super characteristic to have the ability to put people at ease. You have always had this.

A second thing this race personifies about you is your perseverance. This race was very difficult. It is an endurance race, equivalent to running two marathons in one day. Bikers are forced to endure fatigue for a long time before the finish.

Mike your life has been this way. You have had many difficult things to deal with in your life, but you have endured it and have come out the other side. Endurance is so impressive in people. I feel you have that. You have gotten through the hard things, and now you are living a life that you are happy and are on solid ground. At some points of life we just need to focus to keep breathing. We get through it and then it gets behind us. You are a very good example of that in my life.

A third thing about this race that exemplifies my relationship with you is that you and I rode in together. As your younger brother, I felt it was a very memorable bonding moment. You have always been a big brother to me. When I was a freshman in high school and you were a senior, we both ran track. You were "Big Shoe" and I was "Little Shoe" on the team. We even had some relays together, which were noted in the local papers. We have done much together and I have looked up to you for years.

Recently, we have grown even closer. As Ethan has moved to Utah for college, you have taken special interest in him to support him when Tonya and I couldn't be there. You have driven Ethan wherever he needed to go, have given him a place to stay, and have shown up to watch him run in races. You have been a super uncle to our son during this time. Having my big brother come through for me when I really needed it means the world to me.

I sure love you Mike. I will love you forever!

*Coming into the finish of the Lotoja. After 206 miles it was such
a great feeling to ride in together.*

As brothers we never looked better.

To My Sister Laura

When I was a senior in high school, my girlfriend had left for Europe with her family. With my girlfriend being out of the country and with my high school sports career being limited due to injury, my senior year was not going too well.

Around Valentine's Day, the school hosted a "Sweethearts" dance. With my girlfriend out of town I didn't have anyone to go with, so I decided to ask you to be my date. I was a senior and you were a sophomore. I am sure it wasn't the coolest thing for you but you accepted.

The night of the "date" we both got dressed up to look as good as possible. I gave you a corsage to wear and we were out the door. We went to dinner, and then headed over to the dance. Having one-on-one time with you was different in this setting. It showed that we really cared for one another.

At the dance we got our groove on. At least I thought I had it. When I see videos of me dancing in high school it is a little embarrassing to see my lack of style.

Slow dancing was a good time to talk. What I thought was cool was that neither you nor I cared what other people thought about being each other's date. I remember trying to persuade you to stay away from a certain guy who was after you. He was no good. We just talked about all sorts of things.

When the date was over, I gave you a hug and thanked you. It was one of the greatest experiences I have ever had with you.

One thing this experience reminds me of is how beautiful you have always been. You looked great that night. A date anyone would be proud of. To this day you are a pretty woman. I don't know if you have always known it yourself, the way I have seen it. But you are pretty inside and out. Your beauty on the inside is pronounced most by the way you care for others. You do it without a lot of fanfare. But you have always looked after others.

Which brings me to my second point. At the dance, I was older than you by two years. What I have noticed is you really have a soft spot for older people, especially in the way you care for people as a nurse. Perhaps the most dramatic example is the way you have taken care of our mother. As the primary caretaker of our mom, who began to show signs of Alzheimer's in her 60's, you are so patient, never complain, and have incorporated mom's care into your daily life. We could not have asked for a better situation for my mom than to be with you everyday. I am so grateful for you.

A third thing I love about you is your sense of humor. You have a dry but hilarious personality, especially around guys. Sometimes I watch you interact with dad at the dinner table. You will share an experience from the day and it is truly comical. In telling a funny story, you sometimes allow yourself to be viewed as an airhead, which demonstrates a lot of humility on your part. I watch you do this and I know it is part of your gift of humor— your graceful and respectful way of bringing fun to those around you, and not worrying about your own ego. Being around you always puts a bright spot in my day. It is a joy to laugh with you.

I sure love you Laura. I will love you forever!

I was close to you in high school. You have to like the white 80's tie and pants I am sporting in the photo.

Laura at the FC soccer game to watch Brooke sing the National Anthem. You are always there to support us and are continually at mom's side. You watch mom daily. What a saint.

To My Father-in-Law Fred Barnes

The faucet in our master bedroom had a leak. It was time to call Fred. For the past 18 years you were our on-call handyman. Whenever something broke in the house or on the car I would call you up and it was done. You always told us that not only could you make the repair, but that you would enjoy doing it. So this day was no different. I called you and you came to the house that very day. We were so lucky to have you.

At this stage of your life you had suffered a small stroke and some of your skills had begun to slip. You still knew infinitely more than I, but your decision making processes were not always the best.

That day when you came over to fix the faucets you came downstairs to turn off the main water line. You then went upstairs to fix everything. I was watching some television downstairs and saw you go up and down multiple times. I assumed you were turning the water off then on, and checking things out to see if the leaks were gone.

Well I soon became alarmed when I heard a bunch of swearing coming from the bathroom. Then I saw you walking down the stairs toward the basement completely soaked in water. It was as if he had lost in a water fight on a hot summer's day. You said it was like Yellowstone's Old Faithful in our bathroom because you had forgotten to turn the water back off during a final tweak. I was shocked, but somehow not surprised. You eventually stopped the flow and gave up on the job.

This was the day that I said to myself, 'It was a great run with Fred but from here on out I will need to pay a professional for these types of things.' I was so lucky to have you as long as I did. It had been almost 20 years. What a gift!

This story personifies so much about you. One of the biggest reasons why I love you is that you would fix anything for your kids. You naturally were very handy and would never say no. You would spend hours and hours on a project for us and be fine. You had a good mind for figuring out a mechanical problem and fixing it. Lawnmowers were your favorite. You could take something apart and put it all back together like it was nothing. I have always been impressed with that.

A second thing I love about you is that you are funny. You love to talk to people and you can say some of the most amusing things. There could be a book of quotes from you that would be quite a read. Like when speaking to Ethan in high school, "Did you tell your teachers to go to hell today?" It might not be politically correct but it would be highly entertaining to read.

Our kids will most remember you by the dinner conversations we have had. You have always made a meal more entertaining by some of the outrageous things you might say. Laughter has been a big part of our family and much of it can be attributed to you.

A third thing I love about you is your respect for your heritage. If anyone has spent any time with you they will have heard the story of you coming over on the ship from Germany and eating a bunch of fruit while on the boat. You have told us that story 100 times as if we have never heard it before. You speak of hard bread, marzipan, and other German foods as if they are heaven on earth. You love your German heritage. It is something you are very proud of. It is good for our children to see your pride and respect for your ancestral roots.

A few years ago, our family took a trip with you back to see your hometown in Germany. We saw the house you grew up in and the building your school was held in. Herzogenaurach, Germany is a typical old European charming town. You walked around town with a grin and a spring in your step like you were a little kid. It meant the world to you to share your hometown with us.

I sure love you Fred. I will love you forever!

You were proud of yourself this day!

You never stop entertaining us.

To My Mother-in-Law Ella

Ella, you worked full time for me in my financial planning firm. Your genius was to get insurance cases approved before the monthly pay run. You were an expert at it and would go to untold lengths to make it happen. Almost every goal I set would come down to the last few days before a deadline and you always made it happen. The 17 years of working with you was so important to me.

With the free time you had, most of it was spent serving others. One day you met a lady at church who had a college age daughter who was struggling. You immediately asked if you could help. This girl had come out as a lesbian. Her family loved her, but was not perfectly understanding. This was at a time where same sex attraction was not near as accepted as it is today. She was just alone and needed some guidance. You immediately asked her if you could come visit. You were in your late 60's and this girl was a college student, yet you would visit her a couple times a month to check in. There wasn't any fan fair; no one knew what you were doing. I never even met her myself. This was just someone you told me needed some love. Even though you personally differed with her choice of lifestyle, you felt that, as a child of God, she deserved all the love she could get.

At the end of the day there wasn't some remarkable story to tell. All I know is that the girl felt love from a mentor who had nothing to gain by the relationship but service. The girl felt accepted for who she was.

The story illustrates you perfectly. You are one of the quiet giants out there who does not look for recognition, but goes about your business making a difference to the less fortunate. Your life has been dedicated to showing God's care to those who are in need. You care for them and will go to great lengths to help them feel loved. You have said many times to me, "This person just needs to feel loved." You certainly know how to convey love. You remind me of what Tracy Chapman once said, "I've seen and met angels wearing the disguise of ordinary people living ordinary lives."

A second thing these stories symbolize is the way you love your family. When you worked with me, you were literally the perfect team member except for one area. For years while your grown children were having babies, you would come to me and tell me you needed a week off to go visit your daughter after the birth of a grandchild. I never said no. You were always there for your kids.

Your fun, your entertainment, your happiness is driven by your family and the time you spend with them. Your six children are your joy. When you visit, you are not in the limelight, but are reveling in the chance to spend time together. That literally is all you want. You want to be together.

A third thing I love and respect about you is your humble leadership. With Fred traveling so much in your married life, you became effective at wearing many hats and running a household by yourself. You taught yourself how to run the family effectively, and you later ran my business just as efficiently. Whether it is the financials, the logistics of kids, the cooking and cleaning, the spiritual guidance of the family, you just have a way of taking the lead and directing the family to continue on and move forward. To this day you are the one responsible for Fred, finances, and running the Barnes household. You are a quiet leader and you don't even know it. I love that about you.

I sure love you Ella. I will love you forever!

At the Northwestern Mutual Awards banquet. You are over 70 years old but look like Tonya's older sister. You were always a key leverage for my success at work.

You have always loved the trips with your girls. You are just one of them.

Family Photos Thru The Years

Outer Banks South Carolina in 2005

Grand Teton National Park 2006

Sledding at Woodfill Hill in 2007

Outer Banks, North Carolina family reunion in 2011

Family photo shoot 2012

Alaskan cruise in 2016

Family photo shoot 2018

Bibliographical Notes

Chapter 1

Christakis, N.A. and Fowler, J.H. "The Spread of obesity in a large social network over 32 years," <u>New England Journal of Medicine</u>, (2007) 357, 370-379.

Chapter 2

Duckworth, Angela. <u>Grit: The Power of Passion and Perseverance</u>. Simon and Shuster., 2016

Chapter 3

Swindoll, Charles R. <u>Strengthening Your Grip: How to be Grounded in a Chaotic World.</u> Worthy Publishing., 2015. (p. 107)

Moawad, Trevor. 2020. <u>It Takes What it Takes</u> [www.moawadconsultinggroup.com].

Duckworth, Angela. 2016. <u>Grit</u> [www.angeladuckworth.com].

Chapter 4

Selk, Jason. <u>Executive Toughness: The Mental Training Program to Increase Your Leadership Performance.</u> McGraw-Hill.,2012

Chapter 5

Church of Jesus Christ of Latter day Saints. "Book of Mormon" Mosiah 2:17

Chapter 6

Benes, Ross. "Porn Could Have a Bigger Economic Influence on the U.S. Than Netflix." Quartz (June, 2018) 1-2

Chapter 7

Tsosie, Claire. and El Issa, Erin. "2018 American Household Credit Card Debt Study," NerdWallet, (December 2018), 1-2

Daniel Kahneman and Angus Deaton. "High income improves evaluation of life but not emotional well-being." PNAS Early Edition (August 4, 2010) 1-5

Chapter 8

Human Performance Institute. Sept. 7, 2011 Secrets of High Performers [YouTube]

Chapter 10

Sonnenberg, Frank. 2015. 7 Reasons Why Traditions are so Important [www.franksonnenbergonline.org].

Chapter 11

Achor, Shawn. 2014. Happiness as a competitive advantage. [YouTube]

2019. Dimensionality and Factorial Invariance of Religiosity among Christians and the Religiously Unaffiliated: A Cross-Cultural Analysis Based on the International Social Survey Programme. [www.journals.plos.org]

Chapter 12

Buford, Bob. Halftime: Changing Your Game Plan from Success to Significance. Zondervan., 2008.

Chapter 13

DiSalvo, David. "Study: Receiving a Compliment Has the Same Positive Effect as Receiving Cash," Forbes, (November 2012), 1-2

Index

About The Author

Born in Seattle, David Shuley spent the better part of his childhood in Utah, where he learned to love the great outdoors. After high school, David served a 2-year mission in San Antonio, Texas where he shared his faith with others and developed leadership skills he still applies today. After his mission, David returned to Utah to study history at Brigham Young University. Upon graduation in 1993, David moved to Fort Thomas, Kentucky and began a career with Northwestern Mutual. As he grew his financial services practice, David earned both his CLU designation and CFP Certification. Throughout his work life, David's greatest desire has been to help clients reach their own goals and aspirations. His work ethic and respect from clients has propelled him to national recognition as a leader within his industry.

David and his wife, Tonya, currently reside in Fort Thomas, Kentucky. They have four children: Ethan, Blake, Brooke, and Grace. David can be found serving his community in many different ways outside the office. However, one thing is certain: whatever he is doing will fall in line with his values of faith, family, and outdoor physical adventure!

David Shuley

Made in the USA
Coppell, TX
24 September 2020